Reinventing the Feature Story

Mythic Cycles in
American Literary Journalism

Reinventing the Feature Story

Mythic Cycles in American Literary Journalism

by
Stephanie Shapiro

apprentice
house

Baltimore, Maryland
www.apprenticehouse.com

Apprentice House is an imprint of Resonant Publishing

Edited by Jeffrey Bradley and Morgan Hillenbrand
Editorial assistant: Marion Goodworth
Design by Jeffrey Bradley

First printing
10 9 8 7 6 5 4 3 2 1

ISBN: 978-1-933051-00-0

apprentice
house
Baltimore, Maryland
www.apprenticehouse.com

apprentice
house

Apprentice House is a non-profit activity of the Department of Communication at Loyola College In Maryland. The organization is an activity of an advanced elective in the journalism concentration, Book Publishing. When the class is not in session the publishing activities are carried forward by a co-curricular organization, The Apprentice House Book Publishing Club, which pursues publishing activities through Resonant Publishing, whose principal, Dr. Kevin Atticks, is a member of the Communication faculty. Apprentice House is an imprint of Resonant Publishing.

Apprentice House is just one of many experiential learning opportunities available to Loyola students in all our Communication disciplines: journalism, advertising, public relations, digital media, radio and television, and writing. Students are responsible for manuscript selection, editing, author contact, permissions, pricing, production, design, marketing and publicity. Those who complete the course and other students interested in working for Apprentice House can register for a follow-up Practicum in Book Publishing under the direction of Dr. Atticks.

Board of Advisors
Kevin Atticks, Ned Balbo, Andrew Ciofalo
Jean Cole, Gregg Wilhelm

Student Editors (2004-05)

Jeffrey Bradley '05	Morgan Hillenbrand '05
Christine DeSanctis '05	Patricia McNamara '06
Elizabeth Didora '05	Kathleen Nagle '05
Michael Hilt '05	Kerri Reilly '05
Lauren Galvin '05	Erik Schmitz '07
Marion Goodworth '05	

Contents

Introduction:
Lessons in Conformity

In recent years, a significant subset of narrative journalism has been devoted to intimate accounts of tragedy, fatal disease and struggles against great odds. These stories are calculated to appeal at least as much to the emotions as to the intellect.

A sampling of prize-winning pieces in prestigious competitions includes the story of a woman dying of pancreatic cancer, a mother watching her child's killer die in the electric chair, a boy coping with a disfiguring illness.

The 9/11 attacks and the tsunami that struck Southeast Asia have afforded writers a bounty of additional material from which to craft heartbreaking copy.

Once scorned by the elite press and relegated to the women's pages these tales have become a staple in the most reputable newspapers. Why?

Television, with its melodramatic approach to tragedy, certainly had an impact, as has a greater acceptance of tabloid journalism.

The long view also shows that the latest tide of personal journalism performs the same function as it did more than 100 years ago: It instructs readers on how to weather uncertain times and assimilate into society.

Whether liberal or conservative, newspapers have absorbed the rhetoric of "compassionate conservatism" in stories that use examples of hardship to teach lessons in faith, forbearance and acceptance.

In this study, originally written in 1984, I suggest that literary journalism is primarily a gauge of societal need and a means of social control. It was necessary in the 19th century to update myths underpinning the young nation in language convincing to millions of immigrants.

As they wrote rags-to-riches sagas, cautionary tales and accounts of misfortune, reporter Nellie Bly and others reinforced American values such as self-improvement and spiritual stamina. Endings were not all happy, of course, but they rarely failed to convey a lesson in conduct befitting the nascent "American way."

The New Journalists who came of age in the 1960s and '70s rewrote those lessons even as they dismantled the vestigial traits of yellow journalism. Heeding a revolutionary muse, they were intent on probing what they saw as a smug country's misappropriation of inherently solid values in the service of greed, racism and other social ills.

Today, demographics and national priorities may have changed, but the myths embedded in American journalism continue to revolve around the same themes and for the same purposes. While their editorial pages may skew to a liberal view, mainstream newspapers and media Web sites have again succumbed to a form of storytelling reflective of the United States' shift toward conservatism and conformity.

While the feature stories found in the elite press as well as tabloids and other news sources may bear some stylistic resemblance to New Journalism, their structure, content and morals reinforce traditional values, the same traditional values extolled by conservative politicians, social critics and church leaders.

By recognizing the themes that underlie feature stories as well as the stories' intended lessons, readers will be able to comprehend the profound role performed by literary journalism in defining and indoctrinating the American psyche.

1. Origins

When literary journalism is viewed as an expression of myth its enduring cultural power is revealed. And as national priorities change, so do those of literary journalism in a cycle that corresponds to the progression of myth through its primary, romantic, and consummatory stages.

These three stages of myth, as defined by philosopher Philip Wheelwright,[1] are a useful prism through which to understand literary journalism's changing role in establishing, reflecting and recreating national identity.

According to Wheelright, the "primary" stage of myth establishes our mythic consciousness. In the next, "romantic" stage, "the attainment of an original experience of mytho-poetic insight into the nature of reality becomes less important than fulfilling the social obligations established for the myth and for the priests who keep and ritualize it."[2]

The consummatory stage is characterized by the artist's ability to act "as prophet, rather than as priest or ministrant to his people, shaking minds and hearts with new visions rather than providing customary balm for normal social and personal anxieties."[3] The consummatory mythmaker re-envisions "the cultural archetypes that lie behind the variegated surface of his culture's myth-media."

Each stage of literary journalism is a tool for converting

readers through sensational example to the moral values and social obligations of a particular myth stage. Each stage creates the need for the subsequent one in a continual literary cycle.

In this work, the three mythic stages are used to describe three distinct periods of literary journalism. These stages do not necessarily occur in a single given period apart from other stages. Mythic visions, like all art, can cross over and breed with other mythic visions. At any time, we can find the different myths reshaping our lives and competing with one another for credence.

For the purpose of this study it is essential to stress the commanding trends of the mythic cycle. That way, it is possible to see that each stage of myth aptly represents a unique time in America's narrative history.

Our first American writers established the primary mythic images that were to determine the course of all future literary journalism. In accounts of Indian captivities, remarkable providences and journals, writers invented an American whose compulsive self-examination and search for true virtue became the model for the American heroic quest.

In the 19th century, repetition and revision forced primary literary journalism into a romantic, popular phase. To meet the demands of an industrial society, the heroic quest took the form of the rags-to-riches myth.

The New Journalists instinctively understood that consummatory myth was the logical step away from the romantic myths they rejected as dishonest portrayals of American life. Through revolutionary story-telling techniques and language, writers sought to recreate the consciousness of the primary stage of myth, in which our original values are uncorrupted by the greed-inspired ideals of romantic myth.

To understand more fully the evolution of literary journalism, and its continuing cultural function, it is fruitful to turn to historian Richard Slotkin's discussion of American narrative literature. Through his perspective, we come to see the themes and intentions that underpin all stages of literary journalism in the United States.

> On the whole, the development of narrative literature in the first two hundred and fifty years of American history is one of the best guides to the process by which the problems and preoccupations of the colonists became transformed into "visions which compel belief" in a civilization called American. Repetition is the essence of this process. Certain instances of experience consistently recurred in each colony over many generations; translated into literature, these experiences became stories, which recurred in the press with rhythmic persistence. At first, such repetition was the result of real recurrence of the experiences. The Indian war and captivity narratives, for example, grew out of the fact that many pious and literate New Englanders were continually falling into the hands of the Indians or attempted to explain their actions in battle. Once in literary form, the experience became available as a vehicle for

> justifying philosophical and moral values
> which may have been extrinsic to the
> initial experience but which preoccupied
> the minds of the reading public.[4]

A look at the myths established and perpetuated by journalists can lead to a more trenchant grasp of American civilization, as Slotkin suggests, "Myth provides a useful tool for the analysis of the particularity of a human culture."[5]

It is the ambition of this study to examine literary journalism, more specifically, the feature story, as mythological artifact. As all American literature has evolved, sculpting and sculpted by political, social and cultural currents as it does, so has literary journalism. Like all American literature, literary journalism, as a vehicle of myth, is a useful tool for the analysis of American culture.

As a conveyance of myth, literary journalism is also a gauge of change in American society. When leading social concerns, crises, cultural trends give way to others, either gradually or cataclysmically, so does the function of literary journalism. Constructed for the most part on the tenets of realism, reporters use it as a way to interpret for their readers the nation's changing concerns and ambitions.

Literary journalism is also an exceptionally flexible form, easily molded, whether by conscious or unconscious intent. This study will consider the effect of a writer's intentions on the direction and perception of myth in literary journalism. A writer who is concerned with "elucidating myth" as opposed to "obscuring myth,"[6] has lofty ambitions for his prose that are not always fully realized.

However, the conscious effort to redirect American

mythology by exposing the fatal flaws of the original myth, must be considered in an analysis of the power of narrative to control and define a national mythology. So must the critiques of those who pay tribute to the New Journalists as artists who, as Michael L. Johnson has written, have "blown up the reality balloon of the journalistic scene until the mythic cracks begin to show and reveal the dynamic pattern of a cultural archetype or set of interacting archetypes."[7]

What makes the New Journalists different from their ancestors? Can they actually strip artifice from American society and expose the archetypes that lie underneath, or is this an unachievable goal? What are those cultural patterns they want to reveal; where and when were they established and by whom? What is the relationship of those who initiated those original myths to contemporary journalists?

What is the transforming principle that takes a cultural archetype from a nascent stage to the point where revolutionary journalists have taken it upon themselves to unpeel layers and layers of cultural wallpaper, to expose once again the original images that lie beneath? What is the driving force behind a national mythology that can alternately expose, explain, obfuscate and elucidate a nation's common heritage at different intervals of American history? What triggers the cyclic progression from one stage of myth to the next?

Through consideration of Slotkin and other scholars of myth, literature and communications as well as the literary journalists themselves, a preliminary answer to these and other questions may be found.

The feature story will be used as a model of literary journalism for the purpose of this paper. It is a porous form that easily admits whatever the writer wishes to inject to it. Like literary journalism in general, it reflects and refracts a nation's changing moods and priorities.

The feature story is a useful example as well because its origins can be traced to the first printed expressions in this continent, when writers were hard at work defining what the American experience was all about in sermons, diaries, journals and letters. Thus the feature story form, even in its first, fragmented stage, has been a vehicle for shaping and perpetuating myth in this country. It is also a durable form that has survived all periods of journalistic history in this country.

To define the feature story is somewhat more difficult. In a sense, the form has become all things to all people. Form itself is a clue. According to Helen MacGill Hughes, "The story of greatest human interest, like the literary short story, has form ... as an effect of the arrangement of details as motifs, the story achieves coherence and unity."[8]

As for content, one "how to" textbook is all too simplistic in its definition of the feature story as a "hunk of overheard humanity which may or may not have the news value of the large events appearing on the front page."[9]

Broadly defined, the feature story is a genre whose genesis is found in man's timeless desire to shape and recount tales of human experience. It is the ambition of this study to show as well that early American writings, and the myths they promoted, continue to have a profound influence on how those tales are shaped and recounted.

Chapter One Footnotes

1. Wheelwright, Phillip, "Semantic Approach to Myth," In Sebeok, Myth: A Symposium (Bloomington: Indiana University Press, 1965), Cited in Slotkin, Richard, *Regeneration Through Violence: The Mythology of the American Frontier,* 1600-1860 (Connecticut: Wesleyan University Press, 1973), p. 12

2 *Ibid.*

3. *Ibid,* p. 13.

4. *Ibid,* p. 20.

5. *Ibid,* p. 15.

6. Johnson, Michael L., "Wherein Lies the Value?" *Journal of Popular Culture,* 9 (Summer 1975) p. 139.

7. *Ibid,* p. 140.

8. Hughes, Helen MacGill, *News and the Human Interest Story.* Chicago: The University of Chicago Press, 1940, p. 91-92.

9. Ruehlman, William, *Stalking the Feature Story.* (Cincinnati: Writer's Digest Books, 1978), p. 17.

2. A Vehicle of Myth

Literature has helped to record and shape our national mythology from colonial times through the present. Slotkin marks this historically unique interaction of literature and myth: "Printed literature has been from the first the most important vehicle of myth in American, which sets it apart from the mythologies of the past."[1]

Noting that the colonies were founded in the age of printing, Slotkin describes the impact of the age on settlers:

> Since America turned readily to the printed word for expression and the resolution of doubts, of problems of faith, of anxiety and aspiration, literature became the primary vehicle for the communication of mythic material, with the briefest of gaps between the inception of an oral legend and its being fixed in the public print.[2]

Journalism as a literary form is also a vehicle of myth. Like the novelist and the poet, the journalist is a creator of what Slotkin calls the "artifact of myth – the narrative."[3] One way to understand narrative of fiction or fact, is as an expression of the traditions and metaphors of a particular culture. They transform archetypal myths, fundamental to all humanity, into cultural myths unique to that culture. For example, Richard Dorson lists several themes found in the narratives of America's earliest journalists: "the economics of trade, the religion of providences, the folklore of demonism," and relates how these themes shaped "'the great myth-images of America: a land of boundless reaches, a commonwealth personally blessed by God, a fabled frontier alive with marvels."[4] Slotkin speaks of the American writer as the "intelligent manipulator of media and artifacts" who "controls and directs the developments of myth, limiting or augmenting its power to induce the mythopoetic affirmation in its audience."[5]

The archetypal hero myth, or "monomyth," common to all cultures, has emerged as the myth most illustrative of the American experience. According to Slotkin, the heroic quest is "perhaps the most important archetype underlying American culture,"[6] and appears in American literature in endless variations.

When we consider scholar Joseph Campbell's definition of myth as "traditional metaphor addressed to ultimate questions,"[7] the journalist's role as interpreter and perpetuator of the myth of the heroic quest becomes a critical factor in Americans' translation of myth into action and action into myth. Journalists, intelligent manipulators of media and artifacts that they are, in Slotkin's words, appreciate the potency of metaphor. And because of their concern with what is occurring "now," they mold and renew the monomyth in a much more immediate way than those writers who require long periods of reflection for mythic expression. Journalists are ever ready to bend information into the mythological artifacts that appear in the newspaper. Slotkin stresses that mythic artifacts must bend to evolve with the cultural myths they articulate:

> The legends and stories we commonly call myths are simply the artifacts of the myths, and they retain their mythic powers only so long as they can continue to evoke in the minds of succeeding generations a vision analogous in its compelling power to that of the original mythic poetic perception.[8]

Several scholars of journalism who recognize the literary character of the news stop short of acknowledging what Seymour Krim calls journalism's "mythic propensity."[9] Although she relates recurring motifs in the news to those in folklore and fiction, Hughes does not consider the cultural archetypes that those motifs symbolize. News repeats itself, she contends, not as a process of mythological affirmation, but because "human experience, though varied, is endlessly duplicated, and an individual's unique career is a type when numbers of people are considered."[10]

Recalling stories he wrote while a police reporter in Newark, N. J., critic Robert Darnton cannot bring himself to carry the idea of news as story to its ultimate origins as myth, either, "Of course it would be absurd to suggest that newsmen's fantasies are haunted by primitive myths of the sort imagined by Jung and Levi-Strauss."[11] Author Tom Wolfe, as well, cannot reconcile realism and mythological artifact as mutually inclusive components of the feature article. His opinion is expressed in the imaginary monologue of a spiteful "Neo-fabulist" whose only defense against New Journalists and realism is to "return to those most elemental and pure forms of story-telling, the forms of which literature itself has sprung, namely, myth, fable, parable, and legend."[12] Wolfe concludes that while they may have come first, myth and fable "never stood a chance, once more sophisticated techniques were discovered as a printed literature developed."[13]

Media critic Michael Schudson identifies two journalisms in suggesting "a connection between the educated middle class and information and a connection between the middle and working classes and the story ideal."[14] Admittedly, the *Daily News* and the *New York Times* differ greatly, but Schudson's linking of the educated middle class with information alone ignores the universal need for myth, and the mythological artifacts that appear daily in all newspapers

The refined, erudite tones of the *Times* may disguise its mythic propensities but cannot stifle its inherited techniques of storytelling, through which stories have "reached the *New York Times* from Mother Goose," Darton writes.[15] (Examples of mythic stories appearing in this chapter are culled from another member of the elite press, the *Washington Post*.)

Nor does Lord Raglan, a renowned scholar of myth, regard journalism and myth as a dynamic entity. He argues that myth and history (of which journalism is an instrument) are mutually exclusive. History is "the recital in chronological sequence of events that are known to have occurred,"[16] whereas tradition, including myth, relies on "folk memory," is orally transmitted and consequently is inaccurate. Raglan concludes, "The rapidity with which historical events are forgotten shows how unlikely it is that what is remembered in the form of tradition should be history."[17]

But as the concept of news as story develops, journalism's mythic propensity emerges. Comparing news stories with fairy tales, Gaye Tuchman makes the connection between news and myth, "Both draw on the culture for their derivation. Both take social and cultural resources and transform them into public property: Jack Kennedy and Jack of beanstalk fame are both cultural myths, although one lived and the other did not."[18] Elaborating on these two myths, Tuchman suggests that news stories and fairy tales are more alike than not: "Drawing on cultural conventions, members of Western societies impose distinctions between stories about the two men that obscure their shared features of public character and social construction."[19]

In their study of news and mythic selectivity, scholars John Shelton Lawrence and Bernard Timberg speak of the inseparable course of heroic news and cultural myth. Only upon consideration of the idiosyncratic mythic traditions of a culture can we grasp "the selectivities and conventions through which news acquires its heroic story forms."[20] They assert that "The news industry and the entertainment (mythic) industry are part of the same confluent cultural stream, the latter exhibiting features that are peculiar to Americans."[21] They conclude that mythic adequacy, the "degree to which the features of an event conform to the pre-existing features of a mythic paradigm,"[22] is an important measure of newsworthiness.

A sense of timelessness, the process of repetition, and the affirmation of enduring values are common qualities of myth and the feature story. In the same way that "Once upon a time" invokes the timelessness of a fairy tale, Tuchman observes that a lead invokes the timelessness of a news story: "Ultimately both the fairy tale and the news account are stories, to be passed on, commented upon and recalled as individually appreciated public resources."[23] A feature story, which is not under the same structural constraints as a news story, may even begin, "Once upon a time…"

Campbell's notion that myth is "symbolic of the play of eternity in time"[24] calls to mind the ideas of George Herbert Mead and Stephenson regarding the news reading experience. Mead speaks of the "realm of the reverie," a timeless, dream-like state that conjures "imagined enjoyable results" in the minds of news readers, and which "dictates the policy of the daily press."[25] Stephenson describes "quiet absorption in the news" as "more like being in a trance than being in touch with reality."[26] Reverie, trance, play of eternity in time: all suggest a similar state in which past and future are suspended for the temporal experience of mythic, and thus cultural, renewal.

Myth and news change perpetually to comply with cultural modifications, but the values they espouse remain constant, and are reaffirmed and restated through narrative. Speaking about the development of narrative literature, Slotkin states that "repetition is the essence of [the] process" by which "the problems and preoccupations of the colonists became transformed into 'visions which compel belief' in a civilization called American."[27] Similarly, James W. Carey notes that in reading a newspaper, "nothing new is learned but in which a particular view of the world is portrayed and confirmed."[28]

In Mead's discussion of the nature of aesthetic

experience, he describes recorded history as a pattern that repeats itself in mythology and in the mythological artifacts that eternalize mythology: "All history is the interpretation of the present, that is, it gives us not only the direction and trend of events but it offers us the irrevocableness of the pattern of what has occurred in which to embody the still uncertain and unsubstantial objects we would achieve."[29]

Mead's description of history resembles Slotkin's description of myth as "essentially conservative." Like the "irrevocableness of the pattern of what has occurred," myth's source of power is "its ability to...invoke and relate all the narratives (historical and personal) that we have inherited..."[30] The feature story, as narrative and as mythological artifact, contains the code that dictates and perpetuates the pattern of history.

Although Wolfe argues that realism lies far from the realm of myth, we shall see how the realism of reporters' renderings of an urban odyssey, of a feisty paraplegic's violent death, and of a tragically flawed heroine, draw us closer to the structure of the monomyth. The dialogue, and the everyday behaviors of tramps on the street, of a man who "lived by some code derived from hugging the ground,"[31] and of a refugee from Siberia, recast our abiding myths in contemporary forms. It is important to remember Slotkin's precept that a culture's mythology is vigorous and durable only as long as its artifacts evolve with the culture. Through realism, national myths speak in a contemporary, idiomatic voice that echoes our culture. The myths still breathe.

Journalism's pliancy lends itself structurally to the primary, romantic and consummatory stages of mythic development. Features that read like the early journals of our primary mythmakers, like the legends and sermons of romantic mythmakers, like the epics of consummatory mythmakers are the result of the literary freedoms of New Journalism. Today, journalists are essentially romantic mythmakers, the priests who "fulfill the social obligations established for the myth."[36] They sustain the status quo as they justify the "philosophical and moral values which may have been extrinsic to the initial experience but which preoccupy the minds of the reading public."[37]

Russell Nye points out that the popular artist's product "must show a profit"[38] and so he cannot afford the risk of being anything but a romantic mythmaker. The popular artist, "corroborates...values and attitudes already familiar to his audience; his aim is less to provide a new experience than to validate an older one."[39]

A 1986 chronicle by *Washington Post* reporter Neil Henry of his experience posing as a bum on the streets of Baltimore and Washington is the work of a romantic mythmaker, although he imitates the style of both primary and consummatory mythmakers. For a modern audience, Henry re-creates the heroic quest, which, as Slotkin says, is "among the first coherent myth-narratives formulated by a culture."[40]

Henry's odyssey, as he terms it, was an assignment, not a matter of survival or of revelation. He is neither creator nor prophet. Henry retells a myth to suit our times, but provides no new vision or insight that steers our mythic course in an uncharted direction. Just the same, as hero of his own story, and as a black man exploring the life of urban vagabonds, Henry adds an interesting and relevant twist to the myth of the heroic quest. His quest is made even more absorbing in light of what Slotkin has to say: "At the source of the American myth there lies the fatal opposition, the hostility between two worlds, two races, two realms of thought and feeling."[41] Although he refers to the conflict between white man and Indian, Slotkin's words hold true for the conflict between whites and blacks on another frontier.

In his first installment, Henry establishes his Homeric role with a litany of the trials he will endure, and of the fellow travelers he will encounter:

> The Helping-up Mission is where I spent the first two weeks of an urban voyage as a homeless derelict. During this journey, which ended nearly two months later in Washington, I scavenged for food and sought shelter wherever it was available...
> I met men and women who later would be involved in robberies, murders and other crimes of passion and desperation...
> My pockets were empty, but my mind was swimming with intense feelings of adventure and fear.[42]

Employing most of the literary techniques that Wolfe claims free the writer from myth - scene by scene construction, dialogue, and third person point of view are a few - Henry leads us through a mythic underworld and emerges as an initiate into manhood, who leaves the cold behind and takes refuge in his girlfriend's toasty apartment.

On the street, Henry captures the language, behaviors, and philosophies of an array of vagrants, as do other epic heroes who meet companions on the road. His myth encompasses the fugitive myths of those who never knew the American dream, as illustrated in his conversations with a fellow bum named Willie that took place on the heating grate they called home. After waking up from a night on the grate, complete with visiting rats and uncaring passersby, Henry recalls, "I felt weak from hunger and yet almost superhuman."[43] He sees himself as superhuman, a hero, having survived a night of humiliating discomfort.

Henry's adventure, as it parallels Slotkin's description of the heroic quest, does not champion the cause of his street friends as much as it would appear. The "threat of some natural or human calamity" that Slotkin describes is the threat of bums to the average *Post* reader's way of life. As a romantic mythmaker, a "ministrant to his people," Henry reassures his audience that the tramps pose no threat; they are sad, eloquent men about whom more should be done. But tramps are harmless, should the reader accidentally step on one. In the end, Henry, as priest, gives his audience what they want to hear.

At the conclusion of his quest, Henry runs into Allie, a wanderer with many heroic qualities of his own. Allie alone discovers Henry's identity, and that is only right. Amid the litter and fray of back alleys, it takes one hero to know another. We learn Henry has made it through the fire – as a confederacy of heroes is born.

Another example of the realistic treatment of myth in the *Washington Post* is an account of the life and death of paraplegic Hobart Wilson. The headline charges: "Hell on Wheels." Reporter Chip Brown makes the most of Wilson's singularity in the tale of his demise. Again, it is romantic myth, the retelling of an old story in modern form in which myth not re-envisioned to challenge the assumptions of contemporary society, but reestablished to conform to them.

The story opens like a traditional ballad, sung from one generation to another:

> They laid Hobart Wilson in the ground last week. The people who stuck by him — his mother, his wife, his boy Junebug and a handful of other kin — slid the metal coffin over the tailgate of the family's two-tone pickup truck. Then they drove all night in the rain with the body, 500 wet and winding miles from a small brown house in Silver Spring to a grave beside Wilson's father in Harlan County, Ky.[44]

The techniques of New Journalism re-create for a contemporary audience the broadside ballad, which "enjoyed a long history that began when the folksong was first set in type for sale and ended when the newspaper brought the masses stories based on the news."[45]

Wilson was regarded as "garbage" by everyone other than friends and family; even so, "he was one of a kind, a man of the fiercest pride, a poor, white country boy known as one of the most notorious characters in Montgomery County."[46] Paralyzed as a child when he fell from a tractor, Wilson is an amalgamation of American types: he is an antihero admired for his disreputableness ("His grotesque and comic history of roguish feats would be an achievement even for a hellion who could walk.")[47;] he is a trickster, robbing buildings and leaving behind the "weird, grocery-cart wheel tracks"[48] from the skateboard-like contraption on which he propelled himself. He is also a consummate American, an "adamantly self-reliant man,"[49] who rejects proffers of help and pity.

As such an American, Wilson is a descendent of the frontier hero Daniel Boone: "lover of the spirit of the wilderness, [whose] acts of love and sacred affirmation are acts of violence against that spirit and her avatars,"[50] Wilson departs from Boone in a notable way. On Wilson's arm was a tattoo that said, "Born to Lose." Sure enough, as a paraplegic with legs as thin as "drumsticks," the subject of gawks and smirks, Wilson's retaliations, his violent acts of "love and sacred affirmation" only destroyed him and the stranger he crashed into at 100 mph. Daniel Boone was reborn through acts of violence. Wilson, in his ultimate act of violence, dies. In life and in death he was in the wrong lane.

Whether or not he realizes it, Brown is telling us about the chances for survival of the Hobart Wilsons of suburban D.C. As a romantic mythmaker, Brown, like Henry, tells an enthralling tale without toppling his readers' values.

Felicity Barringer's tale of the life of Tamara Wall, "Flight from Sorrow," also from the *Washington Post*, roughly parallels Raglan's criteria for the "Story of the Hero of Tradition"[51] and as such is a unique portrayal of a contemporary heroine and her quest for success. Like the hero who is "spirited away"[52] after an attempt on his life, Tamara Wall was exiled from her native Germany, sent to a Siberian labor camp and eventually to England as a refugee. There, she was raised by a young woman of no relation to Wall, following the pattern of the hero who is "reared by foster parents in a far country."[53] Wall eventually joined her father in Oregon, and remained silent on the subject of her past, like the hero: "we are told nothing of his childhood."[54] Barringer describes the silence Wall maintained throughout her life in Washington, D.C.:

> Her double life was not a matter of conscious duplicity, but one of willful forgetfulness. In Washington, Tammy Wall had found the perfect place to hide herself. She lived in a city that demands little in the way of a past, asking only a present, and perhaps a future.[55]

When the hero reaches manhood, he "returns or goes to his future kingdom."[56] Similarly, Wall arrives in Washington at twenty two as if she had been "newly conceived." While the hero, "after a victory over the king and/or a giant, dragon, or wild beast, marries a princess... and becomes king,"[57] Wall takes on Washington, works her way through law school, marries, and receives her law degree. Like a king, she commands a large audience of admirers. As an attorney, she "prescribes laws"[58] as does the king until, like the hero who "loses favor with the gods and/or his subjects, and is driven from the throne and city,"[59] Wall is fired from her position as assistant counsel on the House Education and Labor Committee after accompanying Adam Clayton Powell on a controversial European excursion.

The hero "meets with a mysterious death"[60] as does Wall, who dies of cancer at forty seven. Just like the case of the hero whose "children do not succeed him,"[61] Wall's daughter, Cynthia, cannot succeed her as intellectual, lawyer, and socialite. She is mentally disabled and incapable of success by Washington standards.

Wall's story is a fascinating account of a heroine with more than one tragic flaw. Her determination to overcome ghosts from the past and hardship is patterned on one form of the heroic quest – the American success story. But as an individual attracted to the political dynamics of Washington, her story is decidedly not the story of the man or woman on the street, but of one who has succeeded in a professional, upper-middle class, white world. That, in the eyes of the reporter, is what makes the story so unique. That as well, is what separates the life of Tamara Wall from the lives of most others.

As a romantic mythmaker, Barringer spins an engrossing tale, but its significance for the majority of Washington is limited. When the series ran, it was avidly read, but no one could understand why it appeared in the first place. Had it been more than a good story, had it been a relevant story that mirrored the experiences of Washington's diverse population, its appearance would not have been as puzzling. In the following discussion of problems that arise when myth frames news, Lapham names loss of identity as a result of reading so many stories that do not reflect one's own life.

At worst, romantic mythmakers warp the original significance of myth, resulting in the corruption of the "faiths and values that were inherent in the original mythopoetic experience."[62] It is the journalist as romantic mythmaker that Lewis H. Lapham fears. He believes pressure is placed on the journalist to satisfy "the desires of an audience that pays for what it wants to hear and stands willing to accept the conventions proper to its place and time."[63] The outcome is a "mythopoetic interpretation of the facts."[64] In other words, deceit:

> If the media succeeds with their spectacles and grand simplifications, it is because their audiences define happiness as the state of being well and artfully deceived. People like to listen to stories, to believe what they're told, to imagine that the implacable forces of history speak to them with a human voice. Who can bear to live without myths?[65]

Lapham asserts that our need for myth has been exploited by the media to the point where an individual may be "tricked into believing that he has no story of his own."[66] He suggests that as a people without a story we are fodder for the romantic mythmaker/journalist: "The resulting loss of identity leads to the familiar chronicle of confused conflict, which in turn can be reprocessed into tomorrow's broadcast or next year's best-selling novel."[67] Darnton adds to Lapham's theory with his own criticism that "newspaper stories must fit cultural preconceptions of the news. Yet eight million people live out their lives everyday in New York City and I felt overwhelmed by the disparity between their experience, whatever it was, and the tales that they read in the *Times*."[68]

Lapham's critique should not be disregarded; certainly questions and confusions arise when we subscribe to our myths at twenty cents a day, and when consumed, cast them on a yellowing pile. But, in demanding a journalistic standard unconfined by cultural astigmatism, he overlooks the newspaper's other function. It is not only a conveyance of information, but a dynamic medium, which reflects and reaffirms our mythopoetic vision in every issue. A journalist reconstructs mythology as he constructs a feature story, even if it is not done consciously. His work is bound and shaped by the "great myth-images of America," the journalist's role as mythmaker is inescapable.

The examples presented in this chapter demonstrate that even the techniques of news gathering and dissemination are derived from ancient forms of mythic narrative. Henry, emulating Homer, handicaps himself, not with blindness but with a vow of poverty to collect the wealth of experience he would shape into epic form. His destitution, unlike Homer's handicap, is not real, but it admits him to a world otherwise inaccessible. (George Orwell, another inspiration to Henry, also underwent self-imposed poverty to be able to write *Down and Out in Paris and London*.)

Brown's narrative imitates the oral tradition and recalls a rich heritage of mythic ballads. Although Hobart Wilson did live, his life seems as fanciful and incredible as those depicted in earlier ballads. In a sense, the facts of his life are immaterial for the myth of Hobart Wilson, like other myths, will live on regardless of its verity. Whether or not a feature story is true is less important than the myth it perpetuates, to the dismay of Lapham and to the delight of those who seek entertainment and cultural affirmation as well as information in their newspaper.

Barringer did not disguise herself to find her story; nor did she consciously imitate the oral narrative tradition to recreate myth. She did immerse herself in the tale of a woman whose experiences were remarkably true to the pattern of the heroic quest. In Tamara Wall's story, we see not only the inevitable union of myth and the feature story, but the unity of myth and life.

In preserving a particular world view, the journalist as romantic mythmaker frequently passes over the lives of those who do not fit that view in word or in deed. While it is reasonable to seek the stories of consummatory mythmakers whose visions encompass those lost and neglected in romantic myths, it is not reasonable to expect their appearance in the daily press. Myth, as it appears in the newspaper, is a commodity[69] supplied according to public demand. The public does not usually demand startling and revolutionary visions with its morning coffee. Consequently, journalism, as a vehicle of myth, will continue for the most part to update and revise the artifact of myth in a purely romantic, diverting form.[70] But recognition of myth as a commodity does not minimize the undeniable and potent presence of mythological artifact in the newspaper.

Chapter Two Footnotes
1   Slotkin, *Regeneration Through Violence*, p. 19.
2   *Ibid.*
3   *Ibid.*, p. 8.
4   Dorson, Richard M., *American Begins* (New York: Pantheon, 1950) p. 12.
5   Slotkin, p. 15.
6   *Ibid.*, p.10.
7   Quoted by Richard L. Greene in "Myth and Criticism," unpublished manuscript, Wesleyan University, September 1967, cited by Slotkin, p. 14.
8   *Ibid.*, p. 18.
9   Krim, "The Newspaper as Literature." In Weber 9ed.) *The*

   Reporter as Artist, p. 183.

10 Hughes, *News and the Human Interest Story*, p. 211.

11 Darnton, Robert, "Writing News and Telling Stories," *Daedulus*, 104 (Spring 1975), p. 96.

12 Wolfe, "The New Journalism," p. 31.

13 *Ibid.*

14 Schudson, *Discovering the News*, p. 89.

15 Darnton, p. 193.

16 Raglan, Lord, *The Hero: A study in Tradition, Myth, and Drama*, (New York: Vintage Books, 1956), p. 4.

17 *Ibid.*

18 Tuchman, Gaye, *Making news: A Study in the Construction of Reality*, (New York: The Free Press, 1978), p. 5-6.

19 *Ibid.*

20 Lawrence, John Shelton and Timberg, Bernard, "News and Mythic Selectivity": Mayaguez, Entebbe, Mogadishu", *Journal of American Culture*, II (Summer 1979), p. 323.

21 *Ibid.*

22 *Ibid.*, p. 328.

23 Tuchman, p. 5-6.

24 Joseph Campbell, *The Flight of the Wild Gander* (South Bend: Regnery/Gateway, Inc., 1979), p. 16.

25 Mead, George Herbert, "The Nature of the Aesthetic Experience," in A.J. Reck (ed.) *The Selected Writings of George Herbert Mead*, (Indianapolis: Bobbs-Merrill), 1964, p. 302.

26 Stephenson, William, *The Play Theory of Mass Communication*, (Chicago: The University of Chicago Press, 1967), p. 51.

27 Slotkin, p. 20.

28 Carey, James W., "A Cultural Approach to Communication," *Communication*, 2 (1975), p. 8.

29 Mead, p. 298.

30 Slotkin, p. 14.

31 "Hell On Wheels," *The Washington Post*, June 6, 1981, p. A1.

32 Wheelwright, Phillip, "Semantic Approach to Myth," in Sebeok, *Myth: A Symposium* (Bloomington: Indiana University Press, 1965), Cited by Slotkin, p. 12.

33 *Ibid.*

34 *Ibid.*, p. 13.

35 *Ibid.*

36 *Ibid.*, p. 12.

37 Slotkin, p. 20.

38 Nye, Russell, *The Unembarrassed Muse: The Popular Arts in America,* (New York: The Dial Press, 1970), p. 6.

39 *Ibid.*, p. 4.

40 Slotkin, p. 10.

41 *Ibid.,* p. 10-11.

42 "Down and Out," *The Washington Post*, April 27, 1980, p.1A-18.

43 "Down and Out," *The Washington Post*, May 5, 1980, p. A 18.

44 "Hell on Wheels," *The Washington Post*, June 6, 1981, p. A1.

45 Hughes, p. 149.

46 *Ibid.*

47 "Hell on Wheels," *The Washington Post,* June 6, 1981, p. A5.

48 *Ibid.*

49 *Ibid.*

50 *Ibid.*

51 Raglan, Lord, "The Hero of Tradition," in Alan Dundes (ed.) *The Study of Folklore* (Englewood Cliffs, N.J.: Prentice-Hall, Inc., 1965) p. 145.

52 *Ibid.*

53 *Ibid.*

54 *Ibid.*

55 "Flight From Sorrow: The Life of Tamara Wall," *The Washington Post*, May 31, 1981, p. A2.

56 Raglan, p. 45.

57 *Ibid.*

58 *Ibid.*

59 *Ibid.*

60 *Ibid.*

61 *Ibid.*

62 Slotkin, p. 12-13.

63 Lapham, Lewis H., "Gilding the News," *Harper's*, July 1981, p. 32-33.

64. *Ibid.*, p. 33.

65. *Ibid.*, p. 37.

66. *Ibid.*, p. 39.

67. *Ibid.*
68. Darnton, p. 192.
69. The notion of myth as a commodity is not new. RalphWaldo Emerson noted the connection between myth and profit in his journal, "We cannot say what is our mythology. We can only see that the industrial, mechanical, the parliamentary, commercial constitute it." (Journal of Ralph Waldo Emerson, p. 383, cited by Harold Schecter, "Introduction: Focus on Myth and American Popular Art," *Journal of American Culture,* 2:2 (Summer 1979), p. 210.
70. Harold Schechter, "Introduction: Focus on Myth and American Popular Art," *Journal of American Culture*, 2 (Summer 1979), p. 210.

3. A Sensational Beginning

We think of Cotton Mather, his father Increase, Jonathan Edwards, and other early American writers as chroniclers, who not only left invaluable records of the journey from Europe to the New World, but whose interpretation of their trials in the wilderness also established a distinct and enduring American mythology. In their riveting accounts of remarkable providences, Indian wars and captivities, natural wonders and witchcraft, the myth of the heroic quest found its American form:

> The community's development in the New World was seen primarily, not in the physical terms of the chivalric romance, but in terms of a psychological and spiritual quest for salvation in the wilderness of the human mind and soul. The physical world of America was but the physical type of this primary wilderness.[1]

We rarely think of these writers, however, as the nation's first feature writers who established the primary myth-images that were to define and direct national mythology in all subsequent literary journalism.

Scholars of American literature, who have sought to locate "central structuring metaphors" for the American experience[2] have focused mainly on the influence of early American writing in fiction, not journalism. For example, when Slotkin refers to American literature in his explanation of the transition from the primary phase to the romantic and literary phases of myth, he clearly considers fiction[3] alone. Other historians, as well, have shortchanged literary journalism's mythic attributes. Rather than find the mythic thread that links Mather's inflammatory words to the sensational human interest stories that carried the penny press and yellow journalism in the 19th century, and to the flamboyant New Journalism in the 20th century, we are given piecemeal strands of history, none long enough to tie the romantic and consummatory stages of the feature story to their primary source.[4]

The historical perspective of New Journalism critics is equally shortsighted. Wolfe traces the root of his work not to early American journalism, but to the early British novel, eschewing Mather, Bradford, and Winthrop for Dickens and Balzac.[5] Hough acknowledges that New Journalism is "not just a borrowing from writers of fiction," that it, "can be traced backward generation by generation through recognizable journalistic forebears."[6] He goes back only as far as 1839, "when newspapers discovered news in the modern sense."[7] Murphy concludes that only in the late 19th century did scholars recognize the "positive relationship between literature and journalism."[8]

Richard Dorson, on Cotton Mather, provides an exception to this lack of hindsight by telling us what is missing in summary dismissals of Puritan narratives as dour and dull:

Mather had an unerring sense for the human interest story, and some of his yarns read like today's newsstand shockers. If you want sex crimes, war and bloodshed, occult mystery, passionate emotions, hair raising adventure, the Magnalia has them all, told in burning words. Mather had put himself body and soul into the issues of his day. In a word, [he] was a master reporter with a fiery earnestness in place of the newsman's flippancy.[9]

The same reporting techniques employed by reporters today were used by the Puritans to record their experiences in logs, diaries, journals, reports, and sermons. Of the remarkable providences, those unusual natural occurrences or human aberrations noted by colonists as signs of God's sanction or wrath, Dorson writes:

> For us the providences possess an entirely unintended interest. Since there were no American newspapers in the seventeenth century, they became our meatiest sources for the news of that day. The providences were carefully recorded by erudite ministers and educated laymen, who double checked them for accuracy with eyewitness testimonies and supporting affidavits. Basically they represent on-the-spot reporting of sensational events.[10]

During the primary stage of literary journalism, there was little or no difference between the literary traditions of fiction and journalism, and the insights gained from examining the feature story's nascent form may scarcely vary from the conclusions of Slotkin and other literary scholars in their examination of indigenous prose fiction. To a certain degree, the two literary genres followed similar patterns of development, as practitioners of both recorded and reflected on the nation's turbulent growth, preoccupied all the while "with the necessity of defining or creating a national identity, a character for us to live in the world."[11]

Although the inherent similarities between fiction and journalism are clearly present, it would not be accurate to contend that what Slotkin and his peers say of literary fiction automatically applies to literary journalism, as well. For all the parallels in form, content and theme, literary journalism's path diverged from fiction as it evolved from the early American narratives because of their common quality: mythic potency.

While myth and literary fiction are generally considered to be compatible, and in fact inseparable in America, myth and journalism are considered to be antithetical concepts, and in their purest form, mutually exclusive.

An author of fiction would never be condemned specifically for the unconscious or intentional adaptation of myth, but journalists whose work reveals mythic scaffolding risk accusations of deceit and inaccuracy despite the verity of their interpretation of events. Only recently, has the "mythic adequacy" of news not been dismissed out of hand as an indication of inaccurate or non-objective reporting, but seriously considered as a vital and intrinsic consideration in news gathering and dissemination, according to Lawrence and Timberg:

> New stories that are "mythically adequate" not only tell us something about the world of events, they also provide confirmation for the faith that we can be finally victorious over the forces that besiege us. Certain kinds of news stories thus take on the character of a ritually structured affirmation of hope. Perhaps the institutions of news, which often style themselves as the enemies of myth, are one of the principal means through which myths are subtly restated and renewed.[12]

Since the institutions that produce news will never admit to "the unconscious but compelling imperatives that shape 'news' in accordance with historically based conventions of mythic narrative,"[13] myth, in journalism, has been forced underground. In contrast to fiction, in which mythic imperative is an acknowledged creative force, mythic expression in journalism is regarded as a problem; as a threat to truth, which journalists, publishers, and media critics must deter with an emphasis on fact, balanced coverage, professional claims for journalism, and a class-bound disdain for the "story ideal." Michael Schudson suggests that unachievable claims for objectivity are used to cover up what amounts to a mythic void in a technical and sterile age:

Objectivity in journalism seems to have been destined to be as much a scapegoat as a belief and more an awkward defense than a forthright affirmation. The belief in objectivity is less central to American journalism than the ground in which it took root. That ground, on which both advocates and opponents of "objectivity" in journalism stand, is relativism, a belief in the arbitrariness of values, a sense of the "hollow silence" of modernity, to which the ideal of objectivity has been one response.[14]

Lawrence and Timberg summarize the inherent contradiction between the two ways of synthesizing the surrounding world, one that relies on the alleged objectivity of fact, or "news;" the other on the subjectivity of story, or "myth":

Like the sociologist Robert Park, most of us want our media to distinguish between "fact" and "fiction," between "news" and "story." A rational, adaptive response to the world seems to demand that we avoid any mixture of objective reality and wish-fulfilling fantasy, that we exclude selective tendencies or projections rooted in personal and cultural preferences. Park judged that the print media of his time – then in the twilight of their dominance – had systematically confused and obliterated such distinctions.[15]

The nagging conflict between fact and fiction, perpetually debated in critical circles, has its root in the clash between the two ways of knowing that inform American primary mythology: the "brain knowledge" of the European Colonists, and the "blood knowledge" of American Indians. This perennial debate, as it turns out, is not just an argument over techniques of fact and fiction, which has culminated in the tepid definitions of New Journalism reviewed in the first chapter. The debate is actually the legacy of the cultural conflict between the Indians and the first settlers, which forms the core of American mythology. Slotkin's citation of D.H. Lawrence's explanation of the "intensity and significance of the white-Indian conflict"[16] is imperative for comprehending that America's most fundamental and internal conflicts determined not only the national mythology, but also the modes of expression used to convey and perpetuate that mythology:

> The blood hates being known by the mind. It feels itself destroyed when it is KNOWN. Hence the profound instinct of privacy. And on the other hand, the mind and the spiritual consciousness of man simply hates the dark potency of blood-acts; hates the genuine, sensual orgasms, which do, for the time being, actually obliterate the mind and the spiritual consciousness, plunge them in a

> flood of suffocating darkness. You can't
> get away from this. Blood-consciousness
> overwhelms, obliterates, and annuls
> mind- consciousness. Mind-consciousness
> extinguishes blood-consciousness and
> consumes the blood. We are all of us
> conscious in both ways. And the two ways
> are antagonistic in us.[17]

Journalism, as it is designated factual and objective, has been associated in America with mind-consciousness – rational thought – but since its first appearance in the New World, journalism has also been the agent of "blood-consciousness," that is, myth. So literary journalism, even as it has communicated the tension between blood and brain at the base of American mythology, has, as an incipient American literary genre, been internally wracked and challenged by this tension. The same conflict that dictated the form of the American psyche dictated the form of literary journalism. Literary journalism does not merely record American events as they conform to the mythic paradigm, which has as its source the "fatal opposition, the hostility between two worlds, two races, two realms of thought and feeling,"[18] it is itself the literary manifestation of that fatal opposition. With its opposing qualities of allegiance to truth and objectivity, and to its elemental mythic context, the feature story is a metaphor for the clashing worldviews that inform American mythology.

Literary journalism, unlike fiction, which is free to an extent from the restraints of fact, must be faithful to fact to preserve its integrity. Its mythic properties are bound in ways that fiction's mythic properties are not. In this sense, literary journalism, continually forced to reconcile its responsibility to truth and its natural inclination to restate and update myth in modern context (the urge to tell a story) has become, in form as well as content, the fortunate solution to one of America's most profound conflicts.

As literary journalism progressed through the various stages of myth, reporters became increasingly aware of the mythic potential of their subject matter. America, transformed by successive waves of immigrants, the industrial revolution, devastating wars at home and abroad, opposing political movements and emerging regional differences, was plumbed to even greater depths for its mythic material. This exploitation of the nation's rich mythic resources became an increasingly self-conscious act, bringing literary journalism's factual premise and instinctual mythic tendencies into striking contrast.

Like all journalism, early American writing was essentially functional. But, Dorson writes, functional prose did not preclude colorful and decidedly sensational prose – the stuff of literary journalism – if it served the interest of the writer:

> Without a leisure class to patronize literature, or a large literate middle class to be courted, belles-lettres had no chance in the seventeenth century, and not much until the end of the eighteenth. Our early classics therefore were written only on strong urgency, to glorify God and extol the plantations, or ... to consecrate

> a tremendous deliverance. Some of the
> meatiest writing in those dawning years,
> like the Indian treaties, the Puritan diaries
> or the court records of the witchcraft cases,
> was purely functional and never intended
> for public reading.[19]

In even the briefest passages of early American literature, we can discern the roots of the feature story – attention to detail, lifestyle, character, human behavior – and even some of the "techniques of realism" that Wolfe ascribes to New Journalism, including scene by scene construction, third-person point of view, and the recording of "status life" - the way we live. Concrete examples of human transgression or virtue, written in vivid story form, with an introduction, plot development, climax, and denouement, illustrated the writers' preoccupation with self-scrutiny and self-improvement. Their work served to justify the errand into the wilderness, and to display the will of God. Like any reporters worth their salt, Mather, his fellow Puritan scribes and other early American writers left their offices, and observed for themselves the fruits of the American experiment. They would also rely on stringers, friends and correspondents from other parts who wrote of their own regions' natural wonders, remarkable providences, Indian problems and political news. Like reporters, these observers were prompted by a natural and aggressive curiosity:

> All write wholly or in good part from
> immediate experience and observation.
> Beverly and Johnson did not choose, like

Sir Walter Raleigh, to write ancient history. Cotton Mather quoted learnedly on spectral evidence - after he had seen witches. Here is no literature or scholarship bred from philosophic musing and library research (although Mathers and Beverly had access to and used good private libraries), but culled directly from vigorous living.[20]

The same graphic language found in the most lurid features today was employed by Puritans to keep their numbers in the fold, and to warn of the gruesome fate awaiting those who strayed away from the rigid tenets of their faith:

> Many remarkable examples to our present purpose have happened in New England, and more than I shall at present take notice of. All wise men that are acquainted therewith observe the blasting rebukes of Providence upon the late singing and dancing Quakers in signal instances, two or three of which may be here recorded, that so others may hear and fear and do no more so wickedly.[21]

So warns Increase Mather, before telling the tale of a man named Harris who erred fatally by converting to the Quaker faith. Mather quotes from the letter of a friend, who writes in gory detail of Harris' demise, giving a specific example of the "blasting rebukes of Providence," and thus validating through sensational propaganda the Puritan conquest of the New World:

> The next day he was found by the seaside, about a quarter of a mile from the place where his hat and other things were found, but out of the road, with three hole like stabs in his throat, and no tongue in his head, not the least sign thereof, one of his eyes hanging down upon his cheek out of his head, the other sunk so deep in his head that at first it seemed quite out, but was whole there.[22]

The preacher Jonathan Edwards was another master of the sensational. Like all Puritan works, his sermons were functional, but his hellfire rhetoric was not beside his point; rather it was directly to the point. Edward's conscious use of sensational prose to strike terror in the heart of his congregation recalls Wolfe's thoughts on the power of New Journalism, "The most gifted writers are those who manipulate the memory sets of the reader in such a rich fashion that they create within the mind of the reader an entire world that resonates with the reader's own real emotions."[23]

Again, in both early and contemporary literary journalism, function is paramount. For Edwards as well as Wolfe, literature does not make the grade unless it jogs the reader's memory and ignites an emotion that enables the reader to connect with the material. As historian Perry Miller recognizes, effecting emotional apprehension is critical to literary journalism's ability to convey mythic material:

Edwards' great discovery, his dramatic refashioning of the theory of sensational rhetoric, was his assertion that an idea in the mind is not only a form of perception but is also a determination of love and hate. To apprehend things only by their signs or by words is not to apprehend them at all; but to apprehend them by their ideas is to comprehend them not only intellectually but passionately. For Edwards, in short, an idea became not merely a concept but an emotion.[24]

What Edwards saw was that a purely physiological – or as we might say, "aesthetic" – reaction to the emotions must always be made at the cost of the idea; what he insisted upon was that by the word (used in place of a thing) an idea can be engendered in the mind, and that when the word is apprehended emotionally as well as intellectually, then the idea can be more readily and more accurately conceived.[25]

In Edwards' reliance on the Indian captivity narrative, it is possible to see that our first writers not only established the nation's mythic consciousness, but also fell upon a foolproof model for communicating and modifying myth for their, and the country's, many purposes. It is a model critical to all stages of myth.

The Indian captivity narratives, autobiographical

accounts of settlers taken prisoner by Indians and forced to endure excruciating brutalities, illustrates most dramatically the American experience in the wilderness, and is the inspiration for American mythology, according to Slotkin:

> Almost from the moment of its literary genesis, the New England Indian captivity narrative functioned as a myth, reducing the Puritan state of mind and worldview along with the events of colonization and settlement, into archetypal drama.[26]

The captivity narratives became an immensely popular genre adapted not only by Puritan ministers for their own theological purposes, but later by those who exploited the Indian captivity narrative for its dramatic qualities. Lawrence and Timberg observe that showman Buffalo Bill's Wild West show brought the captivity form into the 20th century through the presentation "thousands of times [of] an image of settlers being surrounded and besieged or captured by Indians – to be rescued of course by Buffalo Bill or the U.S. Calvary who always appeared in the nick of time."[27]

From the Wild West show, the mythic pattern of capture, detention and return, in the guise of the captivity narrative grew into "one of the most common themes in movie and television melodrama."[28] It also became, according to Lawrence and Timberg, a variant of the American monomyth, defined in Sheldon and Lawrence's book by that name:

A community in a harmonious paradise is threatened by evil; normal institutions fail to contend with this threat: A selfless superhero emerges to renounce temptations and carry out the redemptive task: Aided by fate, his decisive victory restores the community to its paradisal condition: The superhero then recedes into obscurity.[29]

Today, the captivity narrative remains one of the media's stock story forms. The mythic paradigm is "constantly at work in news consciousness."[30] The paradigm decides what we think is newsworthy and establishes a "rank among news stories,"[31] Lawrence and Timberg conclude.

Studies of mythic adequacy by Lawrence and Timberg, and others, trace myth's role in popular culture from its primary formation in captivity narratives to its contemporary manifestations in the realms of the arts and the media. To fully understand the mythic/thematic link that ties our original mythic expressions to today's popular culture, another factor must again be considered: emotional appeal; the degree of which is a measure of how well a vehicle of myth functions. While often obscured today by the frivolity and commercial orientation of much popular mythic expression, emotional appeal is still at the heart of literary journalism. The process of soliciting the sympathy of readers through emotional appeal is how literary journalism functions.

In this light, we can reconsider Slotkin's suggestion that Edwards exploited the captivity narrative for its sensational potential. His deliberate play on his congregation's emotions, his powers of persuasion were as crucial as invoking myth itself for assuring the myth's survival:

> Jonathan Edwards "Sinners in the Hand of an Angry God" (1748) – The archetypal revival sermon by the most subtle student of the psychology of personal conversion – suggests the relevance of the captivity to the psychology of conversion. Analogies between the captivity and Edwards's sermon are especially interesting because of his "sensationalist" rhetoric; the sermon is designed to impose a series of sense perceptions on the hearer, which will bypass or overwhelm the defenses of his corrupted reason and operate directly on his "affections," thus carrying him into the emotional crisis of religious conversion. This is precisely the way in which myth-tales ... operate on their audiences; and the success of Edwards' sermons is testimony to the evocative power of the captivity-myth imager.[32]

With certain modifications, Slotkin's interpretation of Edwards' gripping power can be applied to all successful literary journalism. As much as it is a vehicle of myth, literary journalism is also an exhortation to conversion, be it spiritual or secular. It is this eminently functional aspect of literary journalism that sets the genre apart from its fictional counterpart. Like myth, emotional appeal also has its graduated levels of consciousness. For the Puritans and other early Americans, it was in fact an appeal to an audience's religious emotions. In the next chapters, we shall see how this appeal was transformed in literary journalism to indoctrinate readers in its romantic period and later its consummatory period.

While Edwards' tactics were geared toward religious conversion, subsequent feature writers were content with more secular conversions in a metaphorical American wilderness – the city. There were conversions nonetheless: to a new way of life, to certain value systems and beliefs, to a particular world view based on quintessential American myths. The emotional exhortations that began with our first writers have never really ceased, but have been steered toward different causes according to the changing needs of the country. The feature story has been transformed in a sense by the changing appeals writers have been compelled to make for their readers' attention and faith.

New journalism's lineage is not as elusive as many may think. To think of New Journalism, and the feature story in general, as the contemporary version of a fiery Puritan sermon or of a remarkable providence or brutal Indian captivity, is not so outlandish, after all. A plea for our belief, for our acceptance of a particular world view is a vital aspect of all effective literary journalism. Essential to the ability of literary journalism to excite our interest and to persuade is its polar appeal to the intellect and to the emotions. It is this combination that Miller asserts made Edwards so convincing, and it is this same combination that characterizes our most memorable literary journalism today. Appeal to the emotions does not have to be made at the expense of the intellect, and vice versa. In this sense, the opposing values of ways of knowing things – "blood knowledge" and "brain knowledge" - are not only compatible, but their joint presence is crucial for literary journalism to be successful as a vehicle of myth. It is this "fatal opposition" that kindled our national mythology in the first place.

During the primary stage, the country's mythic consciousness was not only established, but the method for perpetuating and revising our myths was developed. Later it was honed and refined to meet changing national demands. From the primary we advance to the romantic stage of myth, where literary journalists found a new arena for converting readers to the American way.

Chapter Three Footnotes

1   Slotkin, p. 39.
2   Richardson, Robert, *Myth and the American Renaissance* (Bloomington: Indiana University Press, 1978), p. 4.
3   Slotkin, pp. 12-14, 20-21.
4   The feature story is rarely treated in journalism histories as a coherent art form or as an artifact of myth. It is more commonly referred to in the broader context of all journalism history as a belated annex to the corpus of journalism. The feature story is largely discussed only insofar as it contributes to a particular scholar's historical, sociological or literary schema. See Mott, Frank Luther, *The News in America* (Cambridge: Harvard University Press, 1952); Mott, *American Journalism* (New York: the Macmillan Company, 1950); Kobre, Sidney, *Foundations of American Journalism* (Tallahassee: Florida State University Institute of Media Research; Weisberger, Bernard A., *The American Newspaperman* (Chicago: The University of Chicago Press, 1961); Rutland, Robert A., *The Newsmongers: Journalism in the Life of the Nation 1690-1972* (New York: The Dial

Press, 1973); Lee, James Melvin, *History of American Journalism* (Boston: Houghton Mifflin Company, 1923); Cook, Elizabeth Christine, *Literary Influences in Colonial Newspapers: 1704-1750* (New York: Columbia University Press, 1912); Park, Robert E., "The Natural History of the Newspaper," In Wilbur Schiramn (ed.) *Mass Communication* (Urbana: University of Illinois Press, 1972).

5   Wolfe, p. 32-35.

6   Hough, George A., "How New?" *Journal of Popular Culture, IIX* (Summer 1975), p. 117.

7   *Ibid.*

8   Murphy, James E., "The New Journalism: *A Critical Perspective,"Journalism Monograph*, 34 (May 1974), p. 27.

9   Dorson, Richard, *America Begins* (New York: Pantheon, 1950) p. 3.

10 *Ibid.*, p. 10.

11 Slotkin, p. 4.

12 Lawrence, John Shelton and Bernard Timberg, "News and Mythic Selectivity: Mayaquez, Entebbe, Mogadishu," *Journal Of American Culture*, 11 (Summer 1979), p. 328-329.

13 *Ibid.*

14 Schudson, p. 158.

15 Lawrence and Timberg, p. 321.

16 Slotkin, p. 16.

17 Lawrence, D.H., *Studies in Classic American Literature* (New York: Viking, 1961) p. 85, cited by Slotkin, p. 27.

18 Slotkin, p. 10-11.

19 Dorson, p. 130.

20 *Ibid.*, p. 13.

21 Mather, Increase, "Of Railing Quakers," cited by Dorson, p. 122-124.

22 *Ibid.*, p. 124.

23 Wolfe, "The New Journalism," " p. 48 48.

24 Miller, Perry, *Errand Into the Wilderness* (Cambridge: Harvard University Press, 1975) p. 179.

25 *Ibid.*, p. 181.

26 Slotkin, p. 24.

27 Lawrence and Timberg, p. 325.

28 *Ibid.*

29 Jewett, Robert and John Shelton Lawrence, *The American Monomyth* (New York: Doubleday, 1977) p. xx.

30 Lawrence and Timberg, p. 328.

31 *Ibid.*

32 Slotkin, p. 103.

4. Romantic Beliefs

The literary journalism of the 1890s rephrased in contemporary rhythms the nation's original mythic refrains, enabling a new generation of settlers to sing along. The reporters who recorded the tales of tragedy and good fortune in New York City were not conscious artists in the vein of Cotton Mather, who, with his contemporaries, deliberately created primary myth-images and nurtured them in captivating tales of New World experiences. The first settlers had already laid the national mythic foundation; it was no longer necessary in the 19th century to establish the country's mythic consciousness. To keep myth fresh and vital, however, it was necessary to update it in language convincing to the millions of immigrants who were making their home in America.

Romantic literary journalism, as it departed from primary literary journalism, is the focus of this chapter. American mythic expression, through innumerable recastings in the press, reduced the nation's primary mythic images "to an imitable formula, a literary convention, a romantic version of the myth."[1] But just as critical as the changes found in American myth throughout the years are the ways in which its ultimate purpose has remained constant. True to the practical ingenuity of the first printed American literature, romantic literary journalism is essentially functional. Its function is identical to that of primary myth: to convert readers to an American way of life through instruction, example and entreaty. Yet, in the same way that myth shifted from a primary to a romantic orientation according to national demands, the purpose of conversion has also moved from a primarily religious motivation to a more secular and democratic one.[2]

The reporters who translated myth for the scores who entered the United States fit Slotkin's profile of the romantic myth maker, for whom "the attainment of an original experience of mythopoetic insight into the nature of reality becomes less important than fulfilling the social obligations established for the myth and for the priests who keep and ritualize it."[3]

These reporters, who wrote for newspapers like the *World, Sun, Herald* and *Tribune*, adapted original myths to accommodate the needs of a nation of widely disparate terrain, temperament, and ethnic and racial composition. And while not aware, in the same sense as Mather, of their contribution to American's self-concept as it is perpetuated in myth, these reporters were nonetheless conscious of their role as influential public figures, whose profession itself was taking on mythic dimensions. Judging from the unveiled moral lessons and honor of the Puritan work ethic their work included, it is clear that these reporters were self-ordained "priests." It was no longer men and women of the church, but of the press, who kept and ritualized myth in its romantic phase.

In this consideration of romantic mythic expression is an examination of these priests who, beneath their entertaining, and often questionable, accounts of life in the city, delivered sermons suffused with moral guidance and arguments for social conformity in keeping with their public role.

A look at romantic literary journalism must also touch on its commercial qualities. Appearing in newspapers in fierce competition with one another, romantic treatments of myth were calculated to sell. Whether using myth as a commercial commodity worked at cross purposes or in harmony with its other function as a tool for conversion will also be discussed.

Romantic interpretations of myth, on their surface a superficial form of literary journalism, especially when compared to the fiery language and dead earnestness of a Mather or Edwards, have the same intent as America's primary mythic expressions: to reinforce the Puritan-derived notions of self improvement, spiritual rebirth, and acculturation. Romantic literary journalism is actually primary literary journalism adapted to meet the requirements of a young democracy:

> In American society the experience of acculturation and of nation building made this individual experience a social one as well. All men, individually and collectively, were engaged in becoming Americans – in making a new, American identity for themselves and by extension for the whole culture.[4]

As it is in the primary mythic phase, emotional apprehension is the key to conversion in the romantic phase. Newspapers in the late nineteenth century aimed at the unschooled, the immigrants and the laborers. They were brimming with the pathos of poverty, the spectacle of the street, and sudden good fortune or tragedy, all dictated, it seemed, by the invisible rules of fate. Reporters took advantage of the waning Romantic Movement in American literature as well as the budding realism movement to render emotionally gripping feature stories that were simultaneously "real" and thus credible. In their approach, reporters grappled with the two ways of knowing things that form the contradictory nexus of literary journalism – blood knowledge and brain knowledge. Even while recounting a tragedy in melodramatic tones calculated to arouse human interest, reporters also appeared to maintain factual integrity with their use of direct quotes and copious detail.

In the nineteenth century, the Puritan myth of rebirth took the form of the American success story: the rags-to-riches myth. It was the same American myth, in its primary phase, that led a people through the trials of Indian captivities, natural extremes, and illness, weeding out the heretics and the weak along the way. In its romantic phase, the myth would lead them into a bewildering urban environment, where conformity in all capacities was demanded, and for a lucky few, out again, to the company of other self-made men. Like the Puritan elite, who survived God's grueling endurance tests, the heroes who dug out of despairing conditions, outlasted their competition and made it to the top, also became part of the elect. If at one time a sense of well being could be measured according to the degree of one's faith in God, it was now calculated by an entirely different yardstick, as Dorson notes: "Happiness lies not in a state of grace . . . but in property and income."[5]

Yet newspaper owners like Hearst and Pulitzer, who embodied these very success stories, knew their readers well, and realized that only a tiny percentage were destined for even modest wealth. Shrewd businessmen, they were not about to alienate their audience by exalting the rich at the expense of the struggling masses. As a result, the rags-to-riches myth is rarely confronted directly in newspaper feature stories of the time, but referred to obliquely, or rejected out of hand in favor of heroic treatments of the common person.

For example, in a profile of imprisoned labor leader Eugene Debs, sob sister Nellie Bly compares him favorably with his ideological enemies, and living embodiments of the rags-to-riches myth, George M. Pullman and Andrew Carnegie. Then she relates this conversation with Debs:

> "Have you ambition to get rich?"
> "Not in the least, if I had to take my choice between being extremely rich or extremely poor, I would choose the latter. I think the very rich deserve pity instead of censure. … Money getting is a disease as much as pareses and as much to be pitied."[6]

In similar righteous passages, as well as in countless tales of married men driven to suicide because they could not provide for their families (a sample headline: "Death the Last Hope . . . Caught in a Highway Robbery … Jim Flower Swallowed Prussic Acid . . . had Struggled Against Poverty and made Honest Search for Work . . . But all in Vain")[7] The *World* recognized the nobility of poverty and the potential for heroism in the disasters of daily life.

Women, although generally depicted as the weaker sex and even more dependent on fate than men, also emerged as heroic figures in the *World's* daily dramas:

> On the second floor of the old-fashioned house No. 235 Third Street, Gustave L. Ederle, the editor of the America Nemzeter, a Hungarian paper, lies dying of consumption. Down in the ground floor his wife – brave, devoted and beautiful – is taking his place, and alone and unaided save by the printers, is doing all the work of getting out the paper, when she is not trying to nurse her husband back to health. (Only six months has Mrs. Ederle been in this country).[8]

They would never see the success and wealth the *World* dangled in front of readers' eyes in regular features about society's latest rage, or Mrs. Astor's trip to Paris for the social season. Mrs. Ederle and her peers, even if they had to kill themselves, scored moral victory through their efforts, and through the measure of their unrelieved despair.

By making them common heroes, the *World* incorporated willing millions into the mythology and thus the structure of American urban life. They were converted, or acculturated to an existence that required their numbers, their pennies and their toil. They, in turn, were encouraged by the honor the *World* and similar papers bestowed upon the working class. It is through stories of the common man, and those fallen men who abused the promise of the New World, that romantic myth speaks most effectively, "At this point the convention has some of the force of myth; the experience it portrays has become an image which automatically compels belief in a culture-wide audience in the view of reality it presents."[9] In these stories of common people, readers could see themselves, thus rendering them more vulnerable to the moral counsel, the rebukes, the Biblical analogies that inevitably accompanied reporters' accounts.

If the *World's* stories do not all have happy conclusions, they are at least morally and culturally acceptable conclusions. They seem to tell the reader that if they endure their trials and attempt to fulfill society's expectations, as did the heroes they read of, they would not be, no matter what the consequences of their efforts, entirely defeated. Like the captivity narratives, in which American's primary myths were first expressed, the stories in the *World* and similar newspapers of that time are about trial, ordeal and rebirth. Slotkin writes that the captivity narratives were "the root of a growing American mythology in which self-transcendence through acculturation"[10] was a basic theme.

In 19th century New York City, newspaper managements, interpreting their audience's thirst for entertainment and relief, took those primary captivity narratives to the romantic stage. Stylized, commercial, self-consciously maudlin, these tales nevertheless were latter-day captivity narratives. They served as examples, as a means of instruction, for those plunging into the figurative American wilderness of the city. With the guidance of the press, readers could learn, as did Puritans reading the original captivity narratives, the lessons of captivity, which if followed could eventually lead to "self-transcendence through acculturation."

Some of the most emotionally exploitative feature stories of the 1890s not only satisfied readers' unbridled curiosity, but also warned in no uncertain terms of the wages of sin; that is, the penalty for staining Americans' public image. In an account of the imprisonment of New York City's corrupt ex-chief of detectives, an anonymous reporter laces her story with Biblical passages as well as unveiled scorn for the unrepentant prisoner. Her tale, before it lapses into an elaborate description of the detective's relatively cozy cell in the Tombs, is an Edwards-esque denouncement of a man unchastened by his own captivity. It is the narrative, in fact, of a failed captivity. The prisoner, Inspector William M. McLaughlin, refused to be converted by his experience, and was only sorry he was caught. The reporter, in her commentary, instructs her audience on how they should react to his deceit. She asserts that he is even lower than the convicted murderer he shares a prison cell with, because he has "betrayed his sworn trust, [turned] against our citizens the very power and authority vested in him, to be used to protect them."[11]

The reader is exhorted to convert obediently and lawfully to the American mainstream, and to assist in casting out all those sinners who threaten the American way of life. In the same way as Puritans, in their literature, turned out those who subscribed to other beliefs or failed to live up to the Puritan doctrine, this reporter in 1895 is eliminating McLaughlin from what Mather called, "the grace of Heaven."[12] And, like Mather and his brethren, she drives the lesson home with emotional rhetoric, and an unsubtle admonition for other would-be violators of the public trust:

But even if he escapes State prison, his career
is ended. If he had been an honest man he
would now be the Chief of Police. For he
was the logical successor of Supt. Byrnes.
Now he is disgraced, despised, a criminal, a
man who has ruined every prospect in life.
These thoughts passed irresistibly through
my mind as I stood at the grated cell-
door and   looked in at McLaughlin. If
ever there was a great moral lesson for the
public, it is to be found in the downfall
of McLaughlin. Surely, "THE WAY OF
TRANSGRESSORS IS HARD."[13]

The reporter quotes from the Bible, not to directly assert
that the inspector has been effectively banned from Heaven,
but that his career is ruined. The underlying assumption,
of course, is that McLaughlin will not make it through the
pearly gates. Instead of making just that point, the reporter
conjures up a more immediate and timely form of eternal
damnation – a lifelong exclusion from society and a forfeited
opportunity to become chief of police, the highest level
of success he might otherwise have enjoyed. In romantic
mythic expression, as in the story of the crooked detective,
the fear of hell that kept Puritans in line is brought down to
earth and made tangible. The rewards of a life industriously
and reverently spent are also more concrete in the romantic
stage of myth. In an industrial era, when acquisition of
material goods seemed, at least superficially, more crucial
than the acquisition of spiritual equanimity, explaining
heaven and hell in terms of earthly desires made them more

easily understood. Not only is myth itself a commodity in its romantic stage, but the ambitions it seeks to instill in readers are themselves commercial and materialistic.

The reporter also plays upon the equivocal feelings she and her readers have toward the detective, lending her story an entertaining and gossipy tone. As much as he is a criminal, McLaughlin is also a celebrity. In insinuations and attention to detail, the reporter not only reveals scorn, but also awe in the presence of this man. There is even reverence in the care she takes to relate his daily ritual. She may as well be describing the routine of an adored Olympic hopeful as an incorrigible criminal:

> As McLaughlin takes no exercise, he purposely eats lightly but has plenty of fruit. To this, and to the fact that he smokes fewer cigars than before his confinement, and also sleeps well, he attributes his good health and spirits. He eats no prison food, all his meals being sent in.[14]

The reporter's scrutiny of McLaughlin's day calls to mind the love/hate relationship the *World* had with the wealthy and the successful. Referred to constantly by reporters, they are openly despised in sensational features about the struggling poor but revered and talked about with respect in the social pages.

After the stern lecture, the reporter regresses into a patently corny account of irrelevant matters, including the names of neighboring cellmates, their crimes and the observation that flowers were banned from the prison because strychnine was "smuggled into the place once in some roses. Thus must the innocent suffer for the guilty."[15] Thus, a blaspheming sermon ends on a frivolous but romantically appropriate note, to the satisfaction of a pious but undiscriminating audience.

In another *World* feature story, the journey from Europe to America is reenacted with a bizarre twist. Implicit in this re-run is a warning for those tempted by the disorderly spectacle of the New World to leave their scruples behind. The account is highly melodramatic and irresistible; it is also an allegory for those of wavering faith who might otherwise topple the moral standards critical for binding together an immense and diverse urban settlement.

The hero of the tale is not the jaunty, handsome Irishman who left his pregnant girlfriend Mary to find a new life in America, but the "ne'er-do-well" uncle who tailed him and on New Year's Day, shot him in revenge for leaving his niece "to bear her burden of impending disgrace."[16] It is a sobering lesson should anyone regard America as release from prior obligations. There is only retribution for those who do not play by the rules and redemption for those who correct those wrongs, as this lead clearly tells us:

> With the dawn of the New Year, William Walsh, weary, broken, and homeless, with nothing but the memory of a deadly wrong to sustain him, completed his mission of vengeance, in the pursuit of which he crossed the ocean and sent a bullet into the body of Patrick McCabe.[17]

The heroic quest across the ocean, the focus of America's mythology, has in this case, backfired. McCabe, the man with promise, with his future ahead of him, violated the laws of morality. Walsh, a loser by the *World's* suspect standards, manages to preserve the laws of morality through his sense of right and wrong. He is a murderer, and yet in the eyes of the *World*, his crime is justified, as it protects against a lawless, atomistic society.

As in the primary stage, providence plays a major role in romantic myth. Now, though, providence is translated into fate, and predestination is not necessarily a determination of who will make it to heaven, but who will meet the man of her dreams and live happily ever after. God, while still present in the moral judgment of reporters, is a little further removed from the romantic street scenes they paint than he was in Puritans' depictions of their daily lives. God is in New York City by proxy, represented variously by well-situated benefactors, unexpected turns of events and chance encounters that could only pop up in the unpredictable jumble of city life.

In the feature story "Miss Mann is Now a Believer in The Fact That Fate Rules Her Destiny," a reporter describes a fortuitous coincidence as an event that could not have happened any other way; it was predestined. Miss Mann, a hard working young woman, was bound for wedded bliss:

> Mrs. Henry Stock, who was formerly Miss Margaret M. Mann of No. 18 West Seventy First Street, is an enthusiastic fatalist. Up to a few months ago she did not even know what fate was, for she met

with a severe accident and was taken in an
almost hopeless condition to her home.
She was the sole support of a widowed
mother and two younger sisters, and their
situation was a desperate one. Then, fate,
in the person of Dr. Henry Stock, appeared
on the scene.[18]

Even in its most conventionalized and romantic form,
the mythology that supported and directed American
society provided the same kind of reassurance to the *World's*
readers as it did for previous settlers. Miss Mann's willing
belief that fate was responsible for her happy destiny was a
function of similar concerns that motivated Puritans in the
wilderness. The Americans who arrived in the tumultuous
cities in the 19th century were as open to conversion as their
predecessors. "The Puritans believed that the sense of grace,
of acceptance by God the Father, grew directly out of such
moments of intense fear, anxiety, and loneliness,"[19] writes
Slotkin after quoting a particularly threatening passage from
"Sinners in the Hands of an Angry God," in which Edwards
warns sinners they "hang by a slender thread."[20] Similarly,
the work ethic and standards of success that immigrants
were taught through the press grew stronger out of their
own fears, anxiety and loneliness. In that state, they were
especially vulnerable to the moral lessons they read in the
World, which like Edwards' sermons provided exemplary
formulas to follow and noted the terrifying consequences if
they did not. But, while all Puritans were expected to obey
religious tenets, there was no guarantee they would go to
heaven for their efforts. Their fate was predestined and could

not be altered through life-long or last minute observances.

In the same way, the *World* called upon all readers to work as hard as Miss Mann, giving all who did a sense of hope that they would be rewarded. However, Miss Mann, as the *World* hastens to suggest, is only one of a lucky few for whom hard work has paid off. In other words, she, too, was predestined for happiness, unlike many others who, no matter how hard they labored, would not experience the same good fortune. But, as in the Puritan community, the chosen, as well as the unchosen, were expected to toil for God and for society, despite the scant chances of making it to heaven or living happily ever after with the man of one's dreams.

In the dawning industrial age, mechanical explanations for unusual natural occurrences were increasingly common, but Judgment Day still loomed large in the *World's* pages, as it had in the Puritans' remarkable providences. Like Cotton Mather, the *World* received news of highly uncommon natural occurrences from throughout the country. While correspondents did not imbue their accounts with God's decisive presence, as did their literary ancestors, they did take every opportunity to suggest that God had a hand in the spectacular phenomena witnessed.

One story from Michigan related the harrowing experience of a steamer whose passengers encountered a blinding and inexplicable bright light that was "Like a Midnight Sun."[21] The light was so bright that "Stewart Walthew, over sixty years old, was enabled to read the Lord's Prayer from the fine print of a Bible without his glasses."[22] Reading between the lines, it is obvious that the reporter is suggesting that Walthew certainly had reason to consult his

Bible for comfort, as would any good Puritan in the same situation.

Although described in detail, there is no explanation for the strange occurrence, other than for one witness to say he thought it was the end of the world. The description itself certainly suggests that the apocalypse was nigh:

> Suddenly a mountain of darkness seemed to arise between the boat and the light, but the blaze was flashed over its top. In a few minutes the mountain sank backward and the lights were seen, still too brilliant for the eyes to endure. At just 2 a.m., by the captains' watch, the lights flashed, there was a terrific rumbling like a quadruple peal of thunder and then the lights disappeared. Almost on the instant, a tidal wave struck the ship and the phenomenon was over. [23]

There appears to be no conscious attempt to frighten readers into faith, merely to entertain them with a sensational adventure story. References to the Bibl, and to the end of the world are for the most part facile literary conventions used to grab attention. But they also serve the more profound purpose as a device of conversion. "Like a Midnight Sun," is, in a sense, a 19th-century remarkable providence, intended to demonstrate the power of God, in an age when scientific skepticism and the Industrial Revolution were gripping the American imagination. The story is almost reassuring in its message that certain forces are still controlled by a higher being, and are thus scientifically inexplicable. The lesson to be gained here as in the seminal remarkable providences, is that God is a force that must be heeded, especially in the unpredictable wilderness of the New World.

Obligated to fact and a Yankee sense of punctuality, the reporter, after his fearful report, concluded with the information that the steamer, despite its unusual deterrence, was only an hour late at port.

Nineteenth-century reporters not only restyled American myth to suit popular tastes, they restyled their own image in the process. In the primary stage of myth its invention was the paramount activity of writers concerned with establishing America's mythic consciousness. Mather, and others, took the raw material of experience and made it not only the basis for a new civilization's mythic bedrock, but the myth itself. They were both the inventors and the discoverers of myth. Nineteenth-century feature writers, on the other hand, already had the myth to work with. They did not create new myths, but continuously reworked the original ones until they were reduced, as Slotkin notes, to imitable formulas. No longer inventors, but improvisers, these reporters also reworked their own image to suit their societal role as mythic designers. As priests and ministrants to their readers, they were equally intent on fulfilling the social obligations established for themselves as well as for their audience. The common man was their subject, around whom they rewrote and adapted America's primary myths. Thus, they assumed the identity of champions of the common man. With this title, reporters earned the credentials to represent and to instruct their audience. Collectively and individually, reporters' self-styled image took on its own heroic quality.

Nellie Bly, in "Her Day of Observation of Brooklyn's Great Trolley Strike,"[24] provides a telling example of a reporter who not only contributed to the identity in progress of America in her profiles of the poor and working class, but to her own persona as a brave and feisty advocate of the downtrodden. Her careful self-portrayals, in turn, helped to glorify the entire image of the journalism profession.

Bly takes an active role in her stories. Her portrait of the violent and prolonged trolley strike is as much the tale of her attempt to speak with trolley officials and striking conductors as it is of the strike itself. In her opening paragraph, Bly lets readers know that she is painfully aware of injustice and its ironic presence in the promised land of America. Her lead does nothing to challenge the American concepts of freedom and opportunity, so she never questions the values underlying American mythology. Instead, she responds with romantic, sympathetic rhetoric to those who continue to live by these values, despite their own unrewarding lives:

> I have spent the day among the strikers in Brooklyn and I am more than ever convinced that something is wrong, not in Denmark, but in the United States, the land of the free and the home of the brave.
>
> I am not a striker; I am not a capitalist; but I am a believer in justice, and I know that, when a sober industrious saving man has worked for twenty-three years for one company, and in that time has not been

permitted to know the difference between Sunday and any other day in the week, and whose only vacation has been one solitary day in the year, losing that day's wages that he might spend the hours uninterruptedly with his wife and children and still that this man, sober, industrious and saving has only been able to earn enough to maintain the plainest life, devoid of everything except the most pressing necessities, then, I repeat, there is something woefully wrong in the whole system of things.[25]

Bly continues to walk through her story, an intrusive "I." She reinforces her affinity with the luckless, pleading ignorance about the trolley crisis, but only because she has just come "from the starving people in Nebraska." A sharp encounter she had with officials is related verbatim, as much a part of her account as the strike. In one passage relating her attempt to speak with strikers she is asked what paper she represented, Bly's reply, *The World*, drew an angry refusal from one official. The readers come to see Bly as a victim as well, an equal among the ranks fighting for justice. Bly elicits as much sympathy for herself as for the strikers through her manipulative play for readers' emotions. Through her own struggle, she is attempting to convert them to the strikers' point of view.

Bly's active role in her own stories, and her biased commentary, were not a violation of journalistic principles in an age when the field's professional tenets were quite fluid. But in such a time, when reporters were not confined by notions of objectivity and distance, reporters naturally tended toward placing themselves front and center in their own tales. Their self-conscious presence in their own stories was the romantic manifestation of the self-consciousness of artists like Mather, who were aware that they were establishing the land's mythic consciousness. In the romantic stage, artists attempted to sell themselves as much as their product. In fact, they were a critical part of their product.

In Bly's copy, we can see the precursor to the New Journalism of the 1960s and '70s, the questioning and probing of long-accepted inequities that have existed in the name of democracy and free enterprise. Bly is no Mailer, no Thompson. She works with the obvious, the tangible signs of a nation's master plan turned sour. Her descendants would penetrate the American landscape more deeply, for indications of failed national ideals that were perhaps flawed from the start. Bly never questions the moral foundation on which the nation was constructed. This was appropriate in the romantic age of myth, when values were generally reinforced rather than challenged. The aim of popular artists "is less to provide a new experience than to validate an older one," Nye reminds us. [27]

Bly's preoccupation with material indications of poverty and depression are also appropriate. She worked in a country where need was not only prevalent, but also stood out in stark contrast in an era when material wealth was a dominant emblem of success. Bly's priorities mirror not only the genuine needs of the poor, but society's preoccupation with outward signs of success as well. This is not to say that wealth was not a major status symbol when Mailer, Thompson and colleagues hit their stride. Unlike Bly, however, they have had the benefit of some 70 additional years of social history to analyze the impact of that glaring status symbol on the national psyche.

Showing a profit was as important for the press in the 1890s as drawing guidelines and offering a sense of hope to dispirited readers. In the romantic stage of literary journalism, the two goals intertwined and became inextricable, and remain so today in the daily press. To sell papers, reporters did not write revolutionary copy or attempt to reconstruct the basic premises of the American dream. Although the *World* took frequent stabs at the wealthy and the powerful, it rarely questioned the basic values of the country. To the contrary, it reinforced those values in stories that were hard to pass up on the newsstand. The argument for conversion in the romantic stage of myth is an invitation to buy not only the ideals promoted in the paper, but the paper itself. Nye's description of the popular artist as one who "corroborates values and attitudes already familiar to their audience"[28] is quite similar to Slotkin's definition of the romantic mythmaker as one who reduces myth to a convention in which the social obligations established for the myth are fulfilled.

Paradoxically, as reporters molded myths to make them commercially viable – to attract readers with a reflection of their own experiences – the myths themselves grew more diffuse and broad to capture ever greater audiences. Hughes took note of this trend: "The feature story is inspired by something that is in the news, but it is an account in which the local and particular aspects are minimized and the subject is expanded to include similar instances so as to be of very general interest."

American mythology, in its primary stage a guiding principle for individuals seeking God's grace, became in the romantic stage the guiding principle for millions. Conformity, the object of romantic literary journalism, came to characterize the genre itself, as it was stretched and generalized to tell the story of so many at once.

Chapter Four Footnotes

1 Slotkin, Richard, *Regeneration Through Violence: The Mythology of the American Frontier*, 1600-1860 (Connecticut: Wesleyan University Press, 1973), p.20.

2 Helen MacGill Hughes' seminal *News and the Human Interest Story* comes very close to recognizing the power of literary journalism to convert readers to a particularly American mythology. The human interest story "perpetuates the news by making it into literature" according to Hughes. Its themes are identical to those in literature only they are written to evoke the sympathies of the common man and woman in an urban world and to acclimatize him to a new culture. Through Hughes' detailed analysis, the feature story emerges as a genre with a history and purpose, which predate the rise of the penny press. But her history is limited to the extent that it serves her argument that popular literature's presence in the press marked the "beginning of sophistication" of the demos. Hughes does not consider the feature story's potentially huge influence on all audiences. Nor does she recognize the early American literary efforts, which introduce the myth-images that have engendered and propelled the human-interest story as we know it. Hughes, *News and the Human Interest Story*, pp. 147-262.

3 Slotkin, p. 12.

4 *Ibid.*, p. 473.

5 Dorson, Richard M., *America in Legend* (New York:Pantheon Books, 1973), p.4

6 "Nellie Bly in Jail - a Chat with Eugene Debs," *The World*, January 29, 1895, p.1.

7   "Death the Last Hope," *The World,* January 29, 1895, p.1.

8   "Nurse and Editor, Too," *The World,* January 10, 1895, p.10.

9   Slotkin, p. 20-21.

10 *Ibid.,* p. 102.

11 "Inspector McLaughlin in his Prison Cell," *The World,* June 16, 1895, p.38.

12 Mather, Cotton, "A Whoredom Unmasked," in Richard M. Dorson, (ed.), *American Begins,* p.118

13 "Inspector McLaughlin in his Prison Cell," The World, June 16, 1895, p.38.

14 *Ibid.*

15 *Ibid.*

16 "Over the Seas to Slay," *The World,* January 1, 1895, p.1.

17 *Ibid.*

18 "Miss Mann is now a Firm Believer in the Fact that Fate Rules her Destiny," *The World,* January 12, 1895, p. 2.

19 Slotkin, p. 103.

20 Edwards, Jonathan, "Sinners in the Hands of An Angry God," cited by Slotkin, p. 103.

21 "Like a Midnight Sun," *The World,* January 29, 1895, p. 1.

22 *Ibid.*

23 *Ibid.*

24 "As Nellie Bly Saw It," *The World,* February 2, 1895, p. 2.

25 *Ibid.*

26 *Ibid.*

27 Russell Nye, *The Unembarrassed Muse: The Popular Arts in America* (New York: The Dial Press, 1970), p. 4.

28 *Ibid.,* p. 6.

29 Hughes, p. 21.

5. A New Conversion

In "The New Journalism," Tom Wolfe boldly claims an entire generation for himself and an elite group of colleagues: "The New Journalists – Para journalists – had the whole crazed Mammon-faced, drug-soaked, Mau-Mau, lust-oozing sixties all to themselves."[1] His audacious seizure of an era, and with it a literary genre, directly challenges the staid journalists Wolfe defies in his essay to prove him wrong. But by his conclusion, it seems only right that the 1960s could belong exclusively to a select few. As Wolfe crowns New Journalism, he crowns the few as well; as consummatory mythmakers whose visions have torn apart the foolish consistencies of romantic myth to expose the incongruous truth behind the American facade. No longer, Wolfe assures us, should readers be content with the standard "beige" journalism that has bleached out the colorful verities of American life. He and his comrades had come along at the ideal moment to depose romantic myth. The New Journalist would act, in Slotkin's words, as "prophet, rather than as priest or ministrant to [their] people, shaking minds and hearts with new visions rather than providing customary balm for normal social and personal anxieties."[2]

The New Journalists instinctively understood that consummatory myth was the logical step away from the romantic myths they rejected. Like primary and romantic myth, the function of consummatory myth is to instruct and to convert through gripping example. Instead of using these tools to indoctrinate readers with the conventional, romantic myths that had influenced journalism for hundreds of years, the New Journalists used them to incite rebellion, to uncover the inherent corruption of the rags-to-riches myth, and to rally readers to new mythic visions.

To accomplish this, the New Journalists could no longer call upon the tired reporting methods that romantic reporters relied on in their unchanging incantation of the rags-to-riches myth. To lead the way to new truths, to enable readers to truly understand the Vietnam War, Las Vegas, Hollywood, the Kentucky Derby, troubled race relations and economic disparity, the New Journalists had to speak differently from other reporters. In speaking in a new way, they took their art to the consummatory level, and brought American myth full cycle. By dismantling the romantic myths that had given the lie to our original values as spoken in primary myth, the New Journalists were invoking the primary stage of myth. They were making a conscious attempt "to recapture the lost innocence of the mythopoetic attitude by transcending the narrative, logical and linguistic forms which romantic mythologizing accepts and utilizes."[3]

According to Slotkin, highly sophisticated societies characteristically foster artists who are keenly aware of the corruption of the modes of belief that underlie their particular society. Their art deliberately cuts through layers of romantic lies to the fundamental myths. Consummatory artists, those who return to their civilization's primary mythic visions, use a radical new language to become reunited with the primary artists who set that civilization on its course. The New Journalists' disgust with the dull prose that smothered our primary truths led them to Mather, Edwards and other Puritan ancestors. At first, it may seem ridiculous to think of Wolfe, Mailer, and Thompson as 20th-century Jonathan Edwardses and Cotton Mathers. How could these mavericks' boasts and obscenities, debaucheries and irreverence be compared in any way with the rigid morality of our national forebears? It can; at the heart of much of New Journalism, including its most extreme elements, is a fundamental morality, guided by a well thought out sense of right and wrong.

Consider, for example, several passages from Thompson's essay "The Kentucky Derby Is Decadent and Depraved." Thompson, in the course of his account, backslides farther and farther into an orgy of drink. Though the young man's boast of endurance keeps him going, a profound shame is also conveyed in his description of the slapstick-like mishaps that befall him throughout the week. And yet, Thompson continues to look elsewhere for the face that was the "symbol… of the whole doomed atavistic culture that makes the Kentucky Derby what it is."[4] He finds that symbol in the person of an old prep school buddy, through whom Thompson personifies the baseness of the rags-to-riches myth:

> But now, a dozen years later, I wouldn't
> have recognized him anywhere but here,
> where I should have expected to find him,
> in the Paddock Bar on Derby Day. . . fat

> slanted eyes and a pimp's smile, blue silk
> suit and his friends looking like crooked
> tellers on a binge. [5]

However, Thompson is careful to note that he is no better than his former friend; he too is decadent and depraved, but at least he is conscious enough to be ashamed. Somehow, the rampant greed and unsatisfied hunger of the errant rags-to-riches myth has deprived those he observes, as well as himself, of the will to bail out of what his colleague Steadman calls "this terrible scene." [6] Thompson rewards Steadman's acuity by abruptly dumping him at the airport, where his self-hatred is deflected on to his British friend.

The journalist rams the big car through traffic and into a spot in front of the terminal, then he reaches over to open the door on the passenger's side and shoves the Englishman out, snarling: "Bug off, you worthless faggot! You twisted pit-fucker! (Crazed laughter.) If I weren't sick, I'd kick your ass all the way to Bowling Green – you scum sucking geek. Mace is too good for you. We can do without your kind in Kentucky."[7]

By the time New Journalism was in full bloom in the 1960s, the United States certainly qualified as one of those highly sophisticated societies that had buried its essential truths beneath mountains of journalistic prose. In addition, the same unrest that drove people to the streets in protest of the Vietnam War and race relations drove writers like Wolfe and Thompson to a new form of journalism that would diagnose the advanced illnesses of this highly sophisticated society.

It would not be possible to infiltrate quietly a

journalistic wasteland and instigate internal rebellion. Like the protesters, New Journalists had to be noisy outsiders who jimmied locks, banged on doors, and occupied the offices of the establishment. To attack the complacent, revisionist journalism they despised, which had become through countless repetition the vehicle for verifying the philosophical and moral value of romantic myth, they had to throw out the usual tools of journalism, as well – the deceptive notion of objectivity, standard summary leads and the static style of news writing in general. By plunking themselves in the middle of their stories, mastering the devices of realism and peppering their narrative with slang, slurs and curses, the New Journalists could transcend the narrative, logical and linguistic forms that sustain romantic myth. That is why Wolfe would begin a story with the ear-splitting cry of a woman prisoner calling to a man on the street, "Hai-ai-ai-ai-ai-ai-ai-ai-ai-ai-ai-ai-ai-ai-ai-ai-ai-ai-ai-ai-ai-ai-ai-ai-ai-ai-ai-ai-ai-ai-ai-ai-ai-ai-ai-ai-ai-ai-ai-ai-ai-aioreeeeeeeeeeeeeeeeeeee!"[8] He even took pains to explain why he did it: "I like the idea of starting off a story by letting the reader, via the narrator, talk to the characters, insult them, prod them with irony or condescension, or whatever. Why should the reader be expected to just lie flat and let these people come tromping through as if his mind were a subway turnstile?"[9]

Journalism is a participatory sport, Wolfe was telling us, not a spectator sport. Until New Journalism's transformation of romantic literary forms into consummatory art, the reader was somewhat of a cipher, a subway turnstile. He was gradually taught through the consumption of newspapers not to question the conventional ways news was delivered to him, and not to muse at length over the unlimited possibilities of journalism as literature. The radical and abrasive new literary form may have been annoying, and even insulting, to conservative readers, but that's because it was intended to be so. If they had not been obnoxious and brash, even sloppy, and at times painfully self-conscious, the New Journalists would not have achieved their goal of dethroning romantic myth. They may have nudged it a bit, but they would not have seized the power, to paraphrase Wolfe.

As in the other two stages of myth, sensationalism and rationalism came together in the works of New Journalists. Their work is also held together by the tension of the "fatal opposition" of brain-knowledge and blood knowledge. While well- researched and rich in detail, the New Journalism also led readers toward conversion to a consummatory view of the world with fiery language and extreme mood swings. But, unlike 19th- century reporters who quickly established affinity with readers, the New Journalists set themselves apart by magnifying their unusual personalities and experiences. Their deliberate alienation from readers also served the intent of conversion. From their readers' safe standpoint, the New Journalist's approach to life was an exciting and alluring alternative to conventional lives led in accordance with romantic myth. As if from another world, Thompson would drop into those lives, for example, with this riveting lead that bid readers to stay for the whole story and open themselves to the possibility of conversion to a new myth vision:

> We were somewhere around Barstow on the
> edge of the desert when the drugs began to

take hold. I remember saying something like "I feel a bit light-headed; maybe you should drive . . ." and suddenly there was a terrible roar all around us. The sky was full of what looked like huge bats, all swooping and screeching and diving around the car, which was going about a hundred miles an hour with the top down to Las Vegas. And a voice was screaming: "Holy Jesus! What are these goddamn animals?"[10]

To call attention to himself, Thompson would also model his endless, screaming headlines on those long headlines that snared readers in the 19th century. Made up of swift sentences, punctuated with exclamation marks, Thompson's headlines generated a sense of energy and importance, and the feeling that his story could not be passed by. From "The Banshee Screams for Buffalo Meat" comes this headline:

Requiem for a Crazed Heavyweight . . . An Unfinished Memoir on the Life and Doom of Oscar Aeta Acosta, First & Last of the Savage Brown Buffaloes . . . He Crawled with Lepers and Lawyers, But He was Tall on His own Hind Legs When he Walked at Night with the King . . . . [11]

Compare Thompson's headline to the headline for Nellie Bly's piece on the striking trolley workers:

AS NELLIE BLY SAW IT

Her Day of Observation of
Brooklyn's Great Trolley Strike
Visited Strikers in their Homes
She Saw the New Men's Barracks and the
Questionable Food Served to Them

COMMENDATION OF STRIKERS' WIVES
Men tell her of the hardships of the Trolley
Services, Why they Struck and Why They Hope to
Win in the End [12]

Bly's headline is tamer than Thompson's, but both supply the reader with just enough information to draw him into the rest of the story. Both heads are unabashedly opinionated, opinion being a much tastier bait than unemotional objectivity.

Romantic myth does not give way easily to consummatory myth, no matter how persuasive its language. For a writer to effect conversion to a consummatory world view, reprogram our entrenched ways of looking at things, is not a simple matter of composing consummatory myth. The audience, where the New Journalists' powers of persuasion are gauged, is not accustomed to revolutionary vantage points, but to comfortable vantage points from which to assess their lives.

It is the consummatory artist's "critical awareness" that forces him to look at society from new and dangerous perspectives, and separates him from those he seeks to convert," [13] Slotkin tells us. First of all, the consummatory artist is aware of "the need for myth as myth," unlike his forebears. In addition, he has the advantage of historical perspective that those who lived before him who came before did not have. The New Journalists, as consummatory artists, were acutely aware of the need for myth as myth. They realized that this country, like all others, would starve without a cohesive mythology, and that it must be revised continually to stay alive.

Although Wolfe ridicules the concept of myth in literature, and isolates it from realism in "The New Journalism," he is very lucid on the need for myth as myth in "The Right Stuff." The pre-fabricated heroism of America's first pilots to rocket to outer space is a glaring example of the demand for myth as romantic myth, Wolfe discovers. In his depiction of the chaotic press conference where the pilots were first introduced, he conveys America's hunger for heroism, and how the press fed on that hunger by making instant heroes of the pilots:

> By the next morning, the seven Mercury astronauts were national heroes, it happened just like that. Even though so far they had done nothing more than show up for a press conference. They were known as the seven bravest men in America.[14]

Wolfe explains as well how the press created this heroic image:

> Without exception, the newspapers and wire services picked out the highlights of their careers and carefully meshed them to create a single blaze of glory. This took true journalistic skill. [15]

In the most intriguing passage about the press conference, Wolfe describes the press' manipulation of the collective needs of a nation for mythic renewal. He also observes that the patriotic stance of the press would largely prevail, even during the Watergate era when investigative journalism unearthed some of the nation's darkest secrets. He may not have realized it, but Wolfe was describing the staying power of romantic myth in a nation preoccupied with social conformity. He was also describing the press that perpetuated the nation's romantic myths as the priests who "fulfill the social obligations established for the myth." In describing the process of romantic myth, Wolfe is displaying his own awareness as a consummatory artist:

> It was as if the press in America, for all their vaunted independence, was a great colonial animal, an animal made up of countless clustered organisms responding to a single nervous system. In the late 1950s (as in the late 1970s) the animal seemed determined that in all matters of national importance the proper emotion, the seemly sentiment, the fitting moral tone, should be established and should prevail, and all information that muddied the tone and weakened the feeling should simply be thrown down the memory hole. In a later period, this impulse of the animal would take the form of blazing indignation about corruption, abuses, of power, and even minor ethical lapses, among public

officials. Here, in April of 1959, it took
the form of blazing patriotic passions for
the seven test pilots who had volunteered
to go into space. In either case, the
animal's fundamental concern remained
the same: the public, the populace, the
citizenry must be provided with the correct
feeling! One might regard this animal as
the consummate hypocritical Victorian
gent. Sentiments that one scarcely gives
a second thought to in one's private life
are nevertheless insisted upon in all public
utterances. (And this grave gent lives on in
excellent health.)[16]

Wolfe goes on to review the mythical aspect of the
space race and the symbolism of launching a man into
space: "The men chosen for this historic mission took
on the archaic mantles of the single-combat warriors of
a long since-forgotten time."[17] Even as he creates New
Journalism as he writes, Wolfe is rejecting the principles of
romantic myth, including, most importantly, the principle
of social conformity. In doing so, he is also explaining
what consummatory artists are up against – generation
after generation of romantic myth that has wedged itself
insidiously into the texture of American life. To make readers
understand that they, too, are part of this great colonial
animal is part of the task of the consummatory artist, which
Wolfe, in these particular passages, is trying to accomplish.

New journalists also ran into difficulties selling their
opinions because they had the advantage of historical

perspective that most people do not. With their aerial view of society, they could compare today with yesterday by juxtaposing the making of one historical era on top of the legacy of another, as if to show we are just retracing what is already past. The New Journalists did not hesitate to tell us what we hate to hear – that the same mistakes are being made repeatedly for the sake of our romantic mythic visions of life.

In "Miami and the Siege of Chicago," an informal history of the Republican and Democratic conventions, Norman Mailer superimposes two historical periods and finds the patterns in Chicago's past that determined the hysteria of the Democratic Convention in 1968. He sees similarities in the slaughter yards and in the minds of native Chicagoans, in the eyes of pigs and in the eyes of police:

> Yes, Chicago was a town where nobody could ever forget how the money was made. It was picked up from floors still slippery with blood, and if one did not protest and take a vow of vegetables, one knew at least that life was hard, life was in the flesh and in the massacre of the flesh – one breath the last agonies of beasts, so something of the entrails and the secrets of the gut got into the faces of native Chicagoans. A great city, a strong city with faces tough as leather hides and pavement, it was also a city where faces took on the broad beastliness of ears, which were dull enough to ignore the bleating of the doomed, noses battered enough to smell no more

the stench of every unhappy end, mouth
– fat mouths or slit mouths – ready to taste
the gravies which were the reward of every
massacre, and eyes, simple pig eyes, which
could look the pig truth in the face.[18]

Wielding their powers of mythic and historical awareness, Wolfe and Mailer are not entirely successful in their mission to convert their audience to their consummatory visions. Their riveting works were not seen by the populace as a way out of the deadly patterns that write and rewrite American tragedies, but as a threat to a traditional way of life. The New Journalists were regarded as warriors out to slay our modes of belief, not as heroes who would return us to our original mythic visions. Their disguise as strident and threatening radicals, who would lead us into the chaotic unknown, rather than back to the original mythopoetic experience, is perhaps too convincing. Their insight and their historical knowledge create "barriers to the acceptance of the vision of the consummatory mythmaker as social mythmakers, since it is the function of myth to provide a formula for credence and faith, not an apparatus for critical analysis." [19]

Along with an enlightened awareness of the significance of myth in consummatory art comes a heightened self-consciousness. In the consummatory stage of myth, the artist frequently plays the leading role in his own work. The work becomes so overwhelmingly autobiographical that it is hard, even impossible, to consider it without considering the artist, as well. The New Journalist's focus on self was an integral and admired element of personal journalism.

In an introduction to Terry Southern's short piece

"Twirling at Ole Miss," Wolfe explains that in journalistic autobiographies, place and moment are beside the point; it is the writer who matters: "The supposed subject (e.g. baton twirlers) becomes incidental; and if the writer has the wit to make his own reactions that fascinating, the reader doesn't care. Hunter S. Thompson is the maestro of this form and calls it Gonzo Journalism."[20]

Scholars like Eason render personal literary journalism academically kosher as well: "Whereas routine journalism bans discussion of the reporter's relationship to organization and event, New Journalism often makes this aspect of reporting its central story." [21]

Southern's account is a good example of the New Journalist who becomes the hero of his own story, which is the account of a heroic quest for consummatory myth. From the start, Southern establishes a self-conscious tone, alerting the reader that this story is about an unpleasant ordeal, a captivity he must endure to test the degree of his enlightenment. It was also a way to perpetuate the myth of the heroic quest by way of his experience: "In my case, it was the first trip south in many years and I was duly apprehensive."[22]

Southern wastes no time before showing us the close relationship between romantic and consummatory myth by ironically noting that he is visiting the Twirling Institute at the University of Mississippi, just down the road from Oxford, William Faulkner's home town, the day after the author's funeral. In Faulkner, he finds a consummatory artist whose concept of race relations grew out of the romantic, backward attitudes of his surroundings. Faulkner's funeral, Southern writes, gave "a grimly surreal aura to the nature of my assignment,...namely to get the story of the Baton Twirling Institute."[23] Faulkner becomes Southern's guardian angel in the story, a consummatory mentor, whom he later seeks in the library.

Southern makes fun of the standard news writing style he bucks in his account, by employing it to describe those people and events that represent the romantic myths he despises. It is as if he is showing us that the purely factual premise of hard news is the breeding ground for romantic myth. After eyeing the pretty but vacuous twirlers, Southern shoves temptation aside and reminds himself: "But no, there was this job o' work to get on with dry, factual reportage – mere donkey work." [24] Southern is suggesting that if he were to depend on standard journalistic styles, he would never be able to tell the truth of the strange scene before him. Straight reporting only hides the truth and protects the guilty and, what's more, interferes with his heroic ambitions as the discoverer of consummatory myth. Such writing would never allow him the hero's voice.

To stress the absurdity of taking the standard prose approach to his subject, Southern does the "donkey work" for a paragraph or two. By merely quoting Don Sartell, the director of the Twirling Institute and a "highly intelligent young man," [25] Southern manages to satirize him. This way, Southern turns this traditional news writing form against the very people and romantic myths it is intended to protect.

As Southern explores the campus, his assignment increasingly takes on the nature of a heroic quest. Each encounter leaves him more discouraged, and bitterly sarcastic. Each encounter makes him look more like a beleaguered hero, held captive by intolerance and stupidity. Southern's heroic quest is a search for a compassion and morality where he can see none, despite Southern's hospitality. Southern's unfortunate discussion with two racist law students sends him back to the alumni house where he turns on the television: "But, I was not destined to escape so easily, for suddenly who should appear on the screen but ol' Governor Faubus himself – in a gubernatorial campaign rant – with about six-cross purpose facial tics going strong, and in general looking mad as a hatter."[26] Southern discovers that he is trapped in an even a bigger hell – although Faubus, a racist, was campaigning in the Arkansas primary, his speech was broadcast throughout the South.

After picking up a Twirling Institute schedule, Southern visits the library where he looks at a first edition copy of Faulkner's "Light in August," and finds "nigger-lover" scribbled across the title page. Southern's stunned realization that he is trapped in an atmosphere of hatred is registered with the irony of a humorous hero: "I decided I must be having a run of bad luck, as a few minutes later, I suffered still another trauma on the steps of the library." He then recounts a conversation with an immaculate "pink-faced man,"[27] who embodies the antebellum South in demeanor and in word.

Southern's "steely Zen detachment" breaks down, and he makes an emotional appeal for the reader's sympathy: "I headed back to the grove, hoping to recover some equilibrium."[28] But, his concentration on the inane twirlers, including one clad in a miniature Confederate flag, cannot ease his disturbed feelings about the campus, and the romantic delusions suffered by all who occupy it. At this pivotal moment, Southern's heroic search becomes successful, because in his recognition of his inability to remain longer on campus, consummatory myth rises from the ashes of romantic myth: "As the evening wore on, I found it increasingly difficult, despite the abundance of cutie-pieness at hand, to string along with these values, and so finally decided to wrap it up."[29]

As he rides through Oxford on his way home, Southern sees the fountain in front of the courthouse, which had caught his eye earlier. It becomes a symbol of the quenching of mythic thirst for Southern, the one cooling source of relief from the outmoded, racist, romantic world of Ole Miss: "I saw the fountain was still shaded, although it was now a couple of hours later than the time before, perhaps it is always shaded – cool and inviting, it could make a person thirsty just to see it."[30]

Southern concludes his autobiographical sketch. In his appalled reaction to the Twirling Institute, he records his own quest for higher moral ground. He never finds it in his surroundings. In his decision to write what he sees with a sense of humor, yet seriously, Southern is generating consummatory myth. At the same time, his art is a way of surviving his trial in Mississippi, and his search for enlightenment is consummated by his autobiography. This is the process of consummatory myth-making in the New Journalism.

New journalists emerged from their odysseys as different men. They were survivors, and as survivors they were not only the creators of consummatory myth, but the consummatory mythic heroes as well. Eason notes that the search for identity of the author "in relation to the break up of a societal consensus"[31] is the cornerstone of myth in the

New Journalism. In this sense, the New Journalist's search for identity within a crumbling culture is the heroic quest incarnate. The heroic quest is the search for a consummatory myth that re-envisions the primary mythic visions of our literary forebears.

The composite of the typical New Journalist, assembled by journalists themselves and friendly critics, is remarkably similar to Slotkin's portrait of the consummatory mythmaker and illustrates how the great expectations for New Journalism as consummatory myth were generated and encouraged. Through critics' praise and journalists' self congratulations, we can begin to understand that the hopes envisioned for New Journalism were based on the cultural need for an irreverent approach to a crazy, singular time in American history.

Need is the genesis of every new phase of myth. From their comments, we can see that critics and scholars cried out for illuminating myth, rather than tired, opaque romantic myth, and that New Journalism was the answer to their prayers. Like all consummatory mythmakers, New Journalists were "aware and capable of articulating the need for myth as myth."

As we read further, we can find other parallels between the consummatory mythmaker, and the portrait drawn of the New Journalist. Consider the comments of Hellman, an enthusiastic New Journalism fan. There is little difference between his characterization of the New Journalist's talents and those of the consummatory mythmaker. He casts them in the same role. Just as the consummatory artist probes "the variegated surface of his culture's myth media," [32] (Slotkin's words) the New Journalist, according to Hellmann, "breaks through the pre-packaged insights and perspectives which permeate the corporate fiction produced by conventional journalism."[33] Hellman further applauds the New Journalists' ability to probe below the romantic layer of myth, saying, "The need to break through the media-created fiction is one of the major motivations and themes of New Journalistic works."[34] The journalist's job is to "penetrate even more deeply into the truth of every story," Krim writes.[35]

Describing consummatory myth, Slotkin writes, "To the extent that consummatory myth making succeeds, it becomes identical in quality, power, and function with primary myth; it may in fact be the primary stage of a new myth evolution."[36] In what looks like a direct response to Slotkin, Hellmann's imagery as he discusses the New Journalist evokes the age of primary myth, when explorers not only penetrated the physical frontiers of the New World, but also the mental and spiritual frontiers of the mind, calling upon experience on one front to serve as an apt metaphor for the other:

> New journalists directly confront the actualities beyond these images and interpret them for us, fulfilling the function of explorers who pass through the frontiers of ordinary experience and then return to tell us what is on the other side.[37]

Hellmann imagines the New Journalist as a pioneer exploring the contemporary American wilderness who for the first time is discovering primary mythic truths. He asks us to regard the New Journalist as a primary mythmaker who, after years of disillusion, is once again establishing the values and standards by which Americans should abide. We are taken figuratively through the mythic cycle by Hellmann going back to the age of primary myth.

Even the New Journalist's quest is described in terms of American mythology. He is the living incarnation of the search for identity, as he follows the pattern of the traditional American odyssey from innocence to experience, moving "past press releases and press agents to penetrate the mysteries behind the appearance." [38]

The making of the New Journalist as a consummatory mythmaker is revealed, as well, in phrases describing what they do when they write. They are "seizing the power,"[39] Wolfe says. They are magicians, Krim writes, creating "the alchemic dream within our grasp – the transmutation of base everyday matter into the poem of life," [40] in other words, the mythology of everyday life.

New journalists are rebels as well, to hear it from those who describe their work in revolutionary imagery. Hellmann writes, "Almost by definition, the New Journalism is a revolt by the individual against homogenized forms of experience, against monolithic versions of truth."[41] In his boundless praise, Krim suggests that the New Journalists did not merely succeed their predecessors, but overthrew them: "By an unexpected evolution – or revolution – the American realistic short story from Stephen Crane to post John O'Hara has now been inherited by the imaginative newspaperman."[42]

John Hollowell writes, "Although the roots for a New Journalism have long been present in American writing, the forces that existed in the '60s fostered a rebellion against conventions and formulas on a wide scale."[43]

The rhetoric of power, revolution and prophecy is still not enough to assure New Journalists of their lofty standing in the literary kingdom. As if to prove empirically their rebirth as heroes, and journalism's reincarnation as consummatory myth, Wolfe and others pinpoint the moment of New Journalism's conception. Wolfe sets the date in 1962 with the appearance in *Esquire* magazine of Gay Talese's piece, "Joe Louis: the King as a Middle Aged Man."

John Hellmann writes a bona fide birth certificate for New Journalism.

> While there are a number of precedents extending back, through history of both New Journalism and prose nonfiction, the beginning of New Journalism and the nonfiction novel (at least as a discernible format) can with some symbolic justification be dated to 1965, the year when Tom Wolfe's "Kandy Kolored Tangerine Flake Streamlined Baby" and Truman Capote's "In Cold Blood" were published. [45]

By grounding their identity in the certitude of an exact birth date, New Journalists and critics were also asserting independence from all literary journalism that had come before. Without this link to the past, it became easier to think of themselves as primary mythmakers, an elite breed imposing a new mythic consciousness on the clean slate of the American mind. It was as if they were saying that for all intents and purposes, that their work marked the beginning of literary history and all which it had been preceded by was immaterial. With a birth date, the New Journalism movement could also rationally prove its existence and that it was not the invention of a cluster of disparate artists clinging to a unifying identity. They were the legitimate progeny of a worthy ancestor. They had a pedigree.

To thoroughly comprehend aspirations for New Journalism it also helps to reexamine the ambitious blueprint established for it. Even in generic discussions of the form, an outline takes shape along the contours of consummatory myth. New journalism's form lends itself naturally to consummatory myth, Eason suggests. Unlike standard journalism, New Journalism communicates through metaphor, "calling attention to itself as symbolic construction, similar to but distinct from the events it signifies." New journalism attempts to go beyond superficial versions of the truth to strike the more profound truths beneath, "Whereas routine journalism treats reports and events as parts of a whole which is distinct from perceptual categories, New Journalism treats events as symbols of some deeper cultural trend, ideology, or mythology."[46] Eason's analysis constitutes a profile of the consummatory mythmaker, one who refuses to speak in the soothing tones of a journalist who reports even the most dramatic world events as if they are logical and preordained. New journalism, he asserts, is a giant step away from romantic literary journalism, in which fate or predestination is a controlling factor in the news. Eason presents the New Journalists as artists who wake readers from their cultural reveries, forcing them to question the way news is interpreted as if by rote in routine journalism.

Johnson, as well, draws the New Journalists as consummatory mythmakers able to "break through to an 'unofficial truth.'" They respond to our need to make sense of the world through "elucidating" rather than "obscuring myth." They reveal the "archetypal and mythic...even artistic dimensions of popular experience, ones through which the reader may evaluate on a fundamental psycho-cultural level the meaning of that experience for himself and his society at large."[47]

With the irreverent and painstaking dissection of New Journalism, Eason, Johnson and others set readers up for revelations never before seen in the daily papers. In their consideration of New Journalism's consummatory powers, they take it for granted that an eye opening experience for Hunter S. Thompson is an eye opening revelation for a reader, as well. At least they assume if the reader is keen he will decipher Thompson's work as a cliché-shattering odyssey. All the romantic notions about ourselves and our country should disintegrate in Thompson's path. Once again, the commotion that whirled around New Journalism tells more about the high hopes held for the form than the form itself. Those hopes are for access to the American psyche, with the New Journalists to show the way.

Despite their failures, New Journalists' attempt to scale the tallest mythic heights is not an aberration or a wrong turn in the evolutionary process of American literature. The three levels of mythic consciousness discussed in this book – primary, romantic, and consummatory – form a natural artistic progression uniquely adapted to American mythic demands. It was a progression set inexorably in motion by a culture obsessed with the manifestation of values imprinted on the American landscape by the first settlers, and destined to become increasingly self-conscious about its triumphs and defeats. Relentless self-examination and search for identity, habits inherited from the Puritans, persist as we seek to understand our civilization.

Nevertheless, if romantic myth has given way to the desire for consummatory myth in literary journalism, it has also paved the way for an exaggerated sense of self-importance. Self-styled heroine Nellie Bly, who did not think twice about boasting in her story of a generous loan she made to a striking trolley worker, set the stage for the likes of Thompson and Mailer, who crave honor by critics, citation by fans, and public challenge from narrow- minded bad guys.

As America has grown more self-conscious about itself, so have some of its artists; to the point where their acute awareness may fatally conflict with their calling. Mather's egotism did not prevent him from laying the country's mythic foundation. In fact; Mather and his peers established the process of "emerging identity" as the crucial dynamic in the nation's mythology. In the romantic era, reporters, as heroes of their own work, served as teachers whom readers could emulate, and their subjects were held up as role models for readers striving to become acculturated to the American way of life. Again, in the romantic stage, writers' prominent place in their own stories did not hinder them, but helped promote their own careers and their professional's reputation as well as meet the perceived needs of the public.

But in the consummatory mythic stage, the writer's dual ambition – to become the hero of one's own art and to speak as a prophet - were not always compatible goals. This is not to say that New Journalists were not instructive, or that they were not consummatory artists. As on all levels of mythmaking, New Journalists responded to a national cry for imaginative interpretations of a confusing and exciting time. Rising to the challenge, they altered the way we saw things, and deciphered the American patterns of thought that spawned a culture that fostered entities as disparate as Las Vegas, Hollywood, the Hells Angels and the Black Panthers. Their method of persuasion was to serve as outrageous tour guides through the landscape of the American psyche. Their hope was that we would not only begin to see the world through their eyes, but grant them a hero's welcome when they returned.

And yet, even as they tried to steer us away from the conventional paths of thought into new dimensions of understanding, New Journalists remain a product of as well as champions of America's fundamental values. They have not let go of the primary mythic promise of a land swelling with opportunity.

Their quibble is with the way those opportunities have been twisted and thwarted, not with the opportunities themselves. Unfortunately, some New Journalists' bloated sense of self- importance and their intrusion into their own myth serves as a vivid example of an errant rags-to-riches myth.

But if they did not always pass the consummatory mythic vision test, Mailer, Thompson, Wolfe and comparable New Journalists have created a fascinating view of the self-perpetuating nature of American myth. From them we learn that the evolution of myth has much to do with writers' inherent understanding of literary journalism's mythic potential, which also helps to explain their own heightened consciousness about their task. To be worthy of their goal of creating literature of consummatory myth quality, New Journalists had to reinvent themselves, as well. They became the beleaguered, sensitive heroes of their own myths and once they captured our attention with their swaggering presence, critics and scholars were glad to acknowledge them in tributes and glowing validations of their work. They called the New Journalists prophets, magicians, revolutionaries.

As they recreated America's quintessential myth of self-creation, New Journalists were actually enacting the myth. They lived the mythic paradigm of self-creation as they wrote. They, like their journalistic ancestors, plunged into captivities, this time willingly. As self-conscious artists, they made their adventures happen unlike Puritans held by Indians against their will. Now, they were held by the decadent and depraved Kentucky Derby, anti-war protests, the world of custom cars, and other cultural phenomena; this time all by their own design. The New Journalists returned from their captivities, perhaps the worse for wear, but clearly different from before. They were initiated.

Even when they did not give us the consummatory visions we have been prepared to expect, New Journalists distilled the essence of literary journalism. By creating and advancing the genre, they recreated and advanced themselves. The act of self-creation and the act of writing about self-creation are fused in the New Journalism. In a sense, there is no distinction between the writer and the myth. The writer is living myth.

Chapter Five Footnotes

1   Wolfe, "The New Journalism," p. 31.
2   Slotkin, *Regeneration Through Violence*, p. 13.
3   Wheelwright, Philip "Semantic Approach to Myth," cited by Slotkin, p. 13.
4   Hunter S. Thompson, "The Kentucky Derby is Decadent and Depraved," in Wolfe and Johnson (ed.) *The New Journalism*, p. 180.
5   *Ibid.*, pp. 184-184.
6   *Ibid.*, p. 187.
7   *Ibid.*
8   Wolfe, p. 16.
9   *Ibid.*, p. 17.
10 Thompson, Hunter S., *Fear and Loathing in Las Vegas: A Savage Journey into the Heart of the American Dream*; (New York: Popular Library, 1971), p.3.
11 Thompson, Hunter S., "The Banshee Screams for Buffalo Meat," in *The Great Shark Hunt* (New York: Fawcett Popular Library, 1979), pp. 579-580.
12 "As Nellie Bly Saw It," *The World*, February 2, 1895, p.2.
13 Slotkin, P. 13.
14 Wolfe, Tom, *The Right Stuff* (New York: Bantam Books, 1980), pp. 99-100.
15 *Ibid.*, p. 100.
16 *Ibid.*, pp. 100-101.
17 *Ibid.*, p. 104.
18 Norman Mailer, *Miami and the Siege of Chicago* (New York: The New American Library, 1968), p. 90.
19 Slotkin, p. 13.
20 Wolfe, Tom, Forward to "Twirling at the Ole Miss," by Terry Southern, in Wolfe and Johnson (ed.) *The New Journalism*, p. 161.
21 Eason, David L., "The New Journalism, Metaphor and Culture," *Journal of Popular Culture*, 15 (Spring 1982), p. 146.
22 Southern, Terry, "Twirling at Ole Miss," from Red Dirt Marijuana and other Tastes, in Wolfe and Johnson (ed.) *The New Journalism*, pp. 161-162.
23 *Ibid.*, p. 162.

24 *Ibid.*, p. 163.

25 *Ibid.*, p. 163-164.

26 *Ibid.*, p. 168.

27 *Ibid.*, p. 169.

28 *Ibid.*, p. 168-169.

29 *Ibid.*, p. 170.

30 *Ibid.*, p. 171.

31 Eason, p. 148.

32 Slotkin, p. 13.

33 Hellmann, John, *Fables of Fact: The New Journalism as New Fiction* (Urbana: The University of Illinois Press, 1981), p. 6.

34 *Ibid.*

35 Krim, Seymour, "The Newspaper as Literature/Literature as Leadership," p. 173.

36 Slotkin, p. 14.

37 Hellmann, p. 139.

38 *Ibid.*, p. 4.

39 Wolfe, "The New Journalism," p. 23.

40 Krim

41 Hellmann, pp. 7-8.

42 Krim, p. 173.

43 Hollowell, John, *Fact and Fiction* (Chapel Hill: The University of North Carolina Press, 1977) p. 36.

44 Wolfe, "The New Journalism," pp. 10-11.

45 Hellmann, p. 1.

46 Eason, p. 146.

47 Johnson, "Wherein Lies the Value?" p. 139.

6. Full Circle

Most debates sparked by the advent of New Journalism stopped short of probing the mythic qualities it shares with all American literary journalism. Intent on legitimizing the art form, scholars and critics trapped themselves in circular conclusions that said very little. Even those who saw New Journalism's capability for piercing the conventional truths of more traditional journalists did not explore why this new form functioned the way it did. Perhaps, as Johnson claims, "New Journalism is elucidating myth as opposed to opposing to obscuring myth,"[1] but why? Eason takes us closer to the answer in his explanation of New Journalism's metaphorical qualities, but what led New Journalists to this "symbolic construction of reality?"[2] What are the traditions and the values that forged New Journalism?

Form not function steered the New Journalism controversy. Left out of the debate was the historical perspective critical to understanding the function of all literary journalism and New Journalism's greater significance as part of that genre.

By looking at literary journalism, including New Journalism, as the artifact of myth, the pitfalls of polemical debate are avoided. Within a mythic framework, New Journalism's historical alliance with all literary journalism is confirmed rather than denied. Polarized stands taken to validate or to decry New Journalism become complementary elements of the same literary organism when its mythic qualities are considered. The tension inherent in literary journalism, between "brain" and "blood" knowledge, intellectual and emotional thought, and information and story, is what holds it together, and preserves its mythic resilience. That New Journalism is a combination of fact and fiction is a given in this regard. It is how fact and fiction operate to instill belief that must be examined further.

With myth as a guiding principle we can also understand how American literary journalism was constantly manipulated to accommodate the changing national needs. More specifically, Wheelwright's concept of primary, romantic, and consummatory myth affords a way of reviewing American literary journalism's mythic progression of pinpointing its distinctive phases, and of determining how each stage of myth prefigured the next. The three eras of myth were a measure of literary journalism's growth as it kept pace with and influenced cultural and ideological change.

When journalism is considered a vehicle of myth, we can also discern the constants and variables that anchor American mythic evolution. Both repetition and change govern literary journalism's course. Our most fundamental national myth, the heroic quest, endures even as it is transformed to withstand the perpetual shock of the new. The American hero has also remained essentially the same throughout the three mythic stages. At the start of his journey the hero is an innocent who uses what he observes and learns from his experience to recreate himself and his followers in the appropriate image of the times. Every time the journey from a state of innocence to one of experience is reworked the result is a new American identity.

But times change, as does the hero, from the inquisitive Puritan wrestling with the wilderness in the primary stage, to immigrant struggling to master the currency of New York in the romantic stage, to enthralled traveler, who in the consummatory stage, sets out to decode national delusions engendered and corrupted by the preceding mythic phase.

The constants of American mythology, (the hero, the myth, and the way myth functions), were determined in its primary phase when our mythic consciousness was first established. Early writers adopted the captivity narrative as the experience most illustrative of their experience in the wilderness. The narratives' heroes not only survived their captivities but came through with their faith in God revitalized. Once in literary form, their ordeals and their initiation into the grace of God served as an implement of conversion for all who read their stories.

In seeking to convert readers, writers like Mather took their cue from the narrative's subject matter - the conflict between the white man and the Indian. Incorporating the conflict in their works they included the two elements necessary for successful conversion - intellectual and emotional apprehension of experience. By fusing these opposing ways of knowing things in their literature writers also rendered literary journalism a metaphor for the clashing world views that inform American mythology. In literary journalism, the classic division between intellectual and emotional apprehension is thus resolved. Not only do the two coexist, they are inseparable.

In the romantic stage of myth, the American hero was transplanted from captivity among the Indians to captivity in the city. There he was challenged again, not only to endure his tribulations, but also to transcend them as a successfully acculturated denizen of the United States.

At this stage, the original precepts of our national mythology were altered to acculturate the scores of foreigners settled in America. If the original values and faiths were modified or even scrapped for the sake of indoctrinating millions to the burgeoning nation's industrial visions, it did not seem to matter. Luring readers with irresistible stories about their peers, reporters taught the working class values vital to a thriving capitalist system that benefit the elite who were destined to succeed. For the majority there was little reward.

The consummatory stage of American myth was a rebellion against the corruption in the romantic phase of the moral values intrinsic to the original myths. At this stage the New Journalists tried to overthrow the rote beliefs and language brought by their romantic predecessors and to convert readers to a vision commensurate in power and purity with our primary myths.

In the consummatory phase the heroic quest becomes a quest for the primary myths. The search for identity is the struggle to reconnect with those original values which, shorn of their Puritanical extremes, are realistic blueprints for those who seek a virtuous life. Mailer, Thompson and Wolfe's records of excess, whether their own or others, is in fact a chronicle of the destructive results of living by the corrupt romantic myths. The New Journalism as such was an attempt to "recapture the lost innocence of the mythopoetic attitude by transcending the narrative, logical, and linguistic forms which romantic mythologizing accepts and utilizes."[3]

New journalists found themselves in a society conditioned by romantic myth to believe itself free of the deterministic forces that controlled our fate in primary myths. The rags-to-riches myth broke free of the concept of predestination to celebrate the concept of free will - anyone who wants to can succeed. Unloosed from its moral restraints, the rags-to-riches myth became the excuse for success at any cost and for a sneering survival-of-the-fittest attitude toward those unable to escape hardship. Puritan ethics were warped to comply with the ideals of big business that promised profits for the few and meager rewards for the many.

There were other manifestations of the romanticization of our national mythology, many of them chronicled by New Journalists as they immersed themselves in Las Vegas, the Kentucky Derby, the counterculture, Vietnam War and issues of race.

The New Journalists, while hardly fire-and-brimstone bible-thumpers, called attention to the license of romantic myth. In a sense they were demanding, however obliquely, a return to a world in which predestination is acknowledged and where the threat of God's wrath controls our excessive tendencies. Thompson clearly suggests at the end of "The Kentucky Derby is Decadent and Depraved" that he is one of the decadent and depraved. Though his sprees are legendary, Thompson's confession that he is no better than the mob bespeaks a desire for some higher form of control. He wants the option of a virtuous path; without God's tempering presence, he cannot have it.

According to Edwards, sin is a deliberate creation of

God. The incentive to develop a conscience cannot exist without the test of temptation and without the promise of deliverance from evil. In many of the worlds visited by New Journalists the concept of sin did not stir in the minds of freewheeling characters featured in their accounts.

Yet even as the concept of sin is mocked in the authors' portraits, we can see predestination in action in the swift tailspins of their subjects who included themselves. In their tales of decadence, the New Journalists were preaching a profoundly moral message. In effect they were asking us to set the original American myths back on course. It would appear there is a bit of Jonathan Edwards in the New Journalist.

Conversion is the motive of consummatory artists. It is not a conversion to distorted romantic myths, but to the authentic myths, which were supported by a well-developed sense of good and evil. Thompson's rampages, Wolfe's extravagant exaggeration and punctuation, and Mailer's wailing self-pity - all constitute an emotional pitch for our attention. They are the authors' tools of conversion, just as their competent and well-researched works are an appeal to our intellect.

Their techniques and goals differed little from those of Edwards and Mather as they used emotional and intellectual means to persuade readers of the need to restore faith in the nation's original moral values and to accept the guidance that a healthy fear of God allows.

Plying the emotions along with the intellect is the key to conversion just as it was in the primary mythic phase. The tools for conversion may vary; Edwards used the "rhetoric of sensation"[4] and Wolfe used the "devices of realism" but their goals are the same.

Another constant in American literary journalism is the writer's self-conscious presence in his own work. To a literary journalist the process of writing closely resembles the process of self-examination which is an integral aspect of the American heroic quest. The exploration, initiation and self-creation that comprise the dynamic of American mythology are also the tools of literary journalism.

More than in hard news, this process reveals itself in the works of literary journalists who are not obligated to stifle personal feelings and opinions. Such journalists not only update and revise American myths when they write, they are enacting those myths. The act of writing about self-creation, (which essentially is the American myth of the heroic quest), and the act of self-creation essentially become one. Thus the New Journalists become heroes of the myths as they rewrite them.

Writers' self-consciousness accumulates with each stage of myth. From their writings, it is clear that Mather and his peers were acutely aware of their self-appointed responsibility to establish and chart mythic consciousness. In the romantic stage, self-consciousness increased to serve an important practical purpose. Cultivating an empathetic image that readers could identify with, reporters like Nellie Bly garnered their trust. With their readers' allegiance, it was easier for reporters to convert them to a newspaper's moral stance, and not incidentally to convince them to buy the newspapers as well, than if they had cultivated an aloof profile.

At the consummatory stage of literary journalism, writers' self-consciousness increased to the extent that their heroic self-portrayals often dominated their own stories. The vivid first-person accounts of New Journalists were attempts to recreate the primary mythic experience of the Puritans. Like their ancestors, they saw themselves as explorers probing the American wilderness, recording remarkable providences and diving willingly into modern captivities with the intention of extracting moral lessons from their experience.

Even if they sunk to unprecedented lows in the course of their cultural journeys, there was a sublime reason for their actions: The New Journalists were offering themselves as examples of the flawed national character. In a way their follies needed no pious conclusions; they were evidence enough of the debasement of the country's primary myths.

The New Journalists deliberately covered the same ground that their romantic predecessors covered with a less critical eye. Where an earlier reporter may have skimmed the surface of Las Vegas, the Derby, a presidential campaign, Hollywood or the Vietnam War, the New Journalists returned with a red pen to scribble the truth over the institutional lies.

It is in the third, most enlightened phase of myth that artists are most keenly aware of the need as Slotkin says, "for myth as myth."[6] In the New Journalism this awareness prompted the writer's starring role in his own work. Because he recognized the need for myth as myth, he was burdened with the responsibility to perpetuate it. Blessed with mythic insight, it is the New Journalist's cultural duty to preserve and renew his mythic heritage. The New Journalist expressed his awareness and carried out his duties by casting himself as his own hero whose search for identity illustrated his search for consummatory myth. At the same time the New Journalist honors himself as one able to oust stale myth and supplant it with the new. He sees the need for myth as myth, the New

Journalist is indeed a hero.

New journalists, however, waged a tough battle for broad public notice of their heroism. Their call to return to the original mythic visions was not recognized as such by most readers. Instead, their flagrant prose posed a threat to the "traditional" values that have been polished by the romantic myths to which we cling. New journalists' visions may predate the false conventional standards of romantic myth, but they were seen largely as insurgents because they threatened the myths that validate our way of life. From a romantic standpoint they were asking us to throw out our conventional means of faith and to embrace an alien call to arms.

It is not surprising that New Journalists, while successfully creating a consummatory myth for the country's consumption, have failed to sell it to most customers. Not many Americans are in the market for a new, improved interpretation of their beliefs. In this sense, it is the nature of consummatory myth not to be adopted in the age in which it is written. Like other consummatory artists, including Herman Melville and James Joyce, New Journalists' works may inherently preclude wide acclaim in their own time.

New journalists' instinctual understanding of the need for myth as myth and their historical vantage point afforded them the enlightenment that their audience may have lacked, but which was required to comprehend their work. By definition, consummatory mythmakers may go unrecognized in their own time. New journalists, despite their literary breakthroughs, may have failed, in their own age at least, to earn popular acceptance.

The stages of development in the evolution of mythology in American literary journalism reflect the changing needs of the nation, as its artists understand them. The Puritans, who huddled together in a strange new land, invented certain myths to keep their numbers away from the atomistic temptations of the wilderness. Their warnings of God's wrath were driven home by the twin whips of sensational language and rational thought.

Writers caught up in the materialistic spirit of the 19th century perceived a need to make those original myths convincing to millions of immigrants. It was to their advantage to secularize and romanticize the myths, to transform the heroic quest into the rags-to-riches myth. They may not have been aware of what they were doing, but these reporters, out of professional and economical necessity, twisted the original myths into something they were not consciously intended to be. It is in this phase that the original values of primary myth were obscured to fulfill the social requirements of an industrial society that subscribed to a "survival of the fittest" philosophy.

In the 20th century, the artists who were to be lumped together as the New Journalists tapped into the country's own instinct for cultural preservation and heard the call for mythic renewal. These writers answered the call and with their work, turn the mythic cycle to the consummatory stage.

Like other consummatory artists, their energized myths were not entirely appreciated. Yet because their documentation of American life achieved the stage of consummatory myth, the New Journalists kept the mythic cycle in motion and sustained the continual process of national self-identity.

By completing a mythic cycle, they also constructed the

primary threshold of another. Now that the height of the New Journalism revolution is past, it is possible to recognize the wave of romantic storytelling that has followed in the form of sentimental features that in large part reaffirm lessons in conformity and acceptance.

Undoubtedly, plenty of literary journalism in the post-New Journalism era is provocative, instructive and even enlightened romantic journalism. Much of it, however, also consists of the conventional prose formulas employed in the indoctrination of readers to a way of life that distorts and obscures the values of primary myth.

In time, the romantic myths engendered at this stage of myth will give way to another generation of New Journalists whose consummatory visions will complete the mythic cycle once again.

Chapter Six Footnotes

1   Johnson, "Wherein Lies the Value?" p. 139.
2   Eason, "New Journalism, Metaphor, and Culture,"
3   Wheelwright, Philip, "Semantic Approach to Myth," cited by Slotkin, p.13.
4   Miller, Perry, *Errands Into the Wilderness* (Cambridge: Harvard University Press, 1975) p.179
    Tom Wolfe, "The New Journalism," in *The New Journalism,* eds. Tom Wolfe and E.W. Johnson (New York: Harper and Row, 1973), pp. 31-36.
5   Wolfe, "The New Journalism," pp. 31-36.
6   Slotkin, P. *Regeneration Through Violence: The Mythology of the American Frontier,* p.13.

About the Author

Stephanie Shapiro is a feature writer for the Baltimore *Sun* newspaper, specializing in regional and national human interest and cultural stories. She has also freelanced for the *Princeton Alumni Weekly*, *Loyola College Magazine*, the *Washington Post*, *The Runner* magazine and the Annie E. Casey Foundation. She spent two years as the visiting journalist at Loyola College in Maryland, and has further experience teaching journalism and writing at the College of Notre Dame, and the University of Maryland.

Stephanie's writing has won accolades from the Washington-Baltimore Newspaper Guild, the Society for Professional Journalism and the Association of Education in Journalism, and has earned the Baltimore *City Paper's* "Best of Baltimore" award.

Stephanie holds an master's degree in journalism from the University of Maryland. She lives in Baltimore with her husband, Tom Waldron, and sons Benjamin and Henry.

Printed in the United States
27845LVS00001B/319-345

9 781933 051000